Bearded Dragons

Complete Herp Care

Philip Purser

Bearded Dragons

Project Team
Editor: Thomas Mazorlig
Copy Editor: Phyllis DeGioia
Cover Design: Mary Ann Kahn
Design Team: Mary Ann Kahn, Patty Escabi

T.F.H. Publications
President/CEO: Glen S. Axelrod
Executive Vice President: Mark E. Johnson
Publisher: Christopher T. Reggio
Production Manager: Kathy Bontz

T.F.H. Publications, Inc.
One TFH Plaza
Third and Union Avenues
Neptune City, NJ 07753

Printed and bound in China,

07 08 09 10   3 5 7 9 8 6 4

Library of Congress Cataloging-in-Publication Data
Purser, Philip. Bearded dragons : a complete guide to Pogona vitticeps / Philip Purser.
p. cm.
Includes bibliographical references and index.
ISBN 0-7938-2887-2 (alk. paper)
1. Bearded dragons (Reptiles) as pets. I. Title.
SF459.L5P87 2006
639.3'955--dc22
2005035327

The Leader In Responsible Animal Care For Over 50 Years!™
www.tfh.com

Table of Contents

Chapter 1

Introducing Bearded Dragons

I f you were to ask what the absolute, all-around best pet lizard available is, you'd get mixed replies. Some folks favor the arboreal geckos, with their sticky toe pads and unblinking stares, while other hobbyists find a soft spot in their hearts for the herbivorous green iguanas, which are peerless in their vibrant emerald and aquamarine hues. Still other hobbyists might suggest the monitor lizards, whose heavy claws and flesh-rending teeth make them the kings of the lizard carnivores. And while all those species are not without their charm, the true answer to our hypothetical question is, without a doubt: the bearded dragon.

Bearded Dragons in the Pet Trade

Hailing from the deserts and semi-arid scrub lands of southeastern Australia, the bearded dragon, *Pogona vitticeps*, embodies all the fine and positive qualities that hobbyists look for in a pet lizard: unique dinosaur-like appearance, ease of maintenance, gentle disposition, manageable size, and a hardy constitution. Not making their presence felt on the US pet trade until the early 1990s, the bearded dragons—or "beardies," as they are affectionately known—have since taken the nation by storm, showing up in pet shops, herp expos, and online in record numbers. Widely bred in captivity, these delightful herps (a term used for reptiles and amphibians collectively) are available for lower and lower prices each year. With every passing mating season, selective breeding produces more and more unusual color varieties. The pastel dragons, for example, have orange heads, but pallid bodies best described as ghostly.

A little over a decade ago, most people would have looked at you sideways had you mentioned your pet beardie, but today, thanks to the tireless efforts of hobbyists and professional breeders, these delightful lizards are common pet store animals. But even the perfect pet lizard cannot care for itself in captivity. In order to thrive in the captive environment, the perfect lizard must be cared for by the perfect hobbyist. When a person makes the choice to purchase a bearded dragon, he or she must consider that that choice amounts to substantial, long-term (in the case of the bearded dragon, sometimes as long as 10 to 12 years) obligations of feeding, heating, lighting, and cleaning an animal that is entirely dependent upon its keeper for all its needs. But all this responsibility should not be seen as drudgery or labor; it should be an

Bearded dragons are bred by hobbyists and commercial breeders by the thousands to supply the demand for this charming reptile pet.

adventure, a romp through the joys of life with a reptilian companion. After all, why else would you buy a beardie if you didn't plan on enjoying the little rascal?

Bearded Dragon Species

The name "bearded dragon," in respect to those animals appearing in the pet trade, refers primarily to the species known as *Pogona vitticeps*, the inland bearded dragon. There are other bearded dragons that have similar habits and lifestyles as the inland bearded dragon. The bearded dragons belong to the family Agamidae, which includes such well-known lizards as

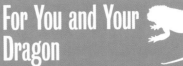

For You and Your Dragon

I wrote this book to help you, the hobbyist, as much as I can through all your ups and downs with your bearded dragon. I've been keeping herps, beardies included, for a long time, and as you read this text, you'll learn the tips, secrets, and time-tested practices that will raise the standard of living for your dragon. The information within this book will help make the years you share with your beardie the best possible.

the uromastyx (also called spiny-tails), water dragons, and the somewhat demonic-looking moloch or thorny devil. The genus *Pogona* (formerly part of the genus *Amphibolurus*) contains eight species of dragons, only four of which appear in the US pet trade, and only two of those with any regularity. All species are arid-dwelling, sun-seeking, heat-loving, omnivorous creatures, and to the untrained eye, differentiation between some of the various species can be very difficult. For our purposes here, the species are described in alphabetical order based on their Latin specific names.

The coastal bearded dragon is very similar in appearance to the more common inland bearded dragon.

Scientific Names

You may have noticed that sometimes there are words in italics that appear after the name of an animal. This is the scientific name, and each animal only has one such name. Biologists determine the scientific name of each animal based on what other animals it is related to. Each scientific name has two parts: The first part of the name is called the genus, while the second part is the species. This combination of genus and species is unique for each animal. Scientific names allow scientists all over the world to talk about each animal without worrying about language barriers or other similar animals being confused with the one they want to discuss.

A scientific name is often abbreviated after the first usage. The genus is abbreviated to the first letter. So, after introducing the bearded dragon as *Pogona vitticeps,* it can be referred to as *P. vitticeps.* If the author is talking about all the lizards in this genus, he or she can use *Pogona* without a species name attached.

Scientific names are used frequently in the herp and the fish hobbies.

Pogona barbata

The largest of the bearded dragon species is the coastal bearded dragon, *P. barbata,* which grows to a maximum of 23 to 25 inches (58.4 to 63.5 cm) in total length. Of course, over half of this length is tail; the body length rarely exceeds 10 to 11 inches (25.4 to 27.9 cm). Found along the eastern and southeastern coasts of Australia, the coastal beardie is a semi-arboreal lizard that frequents residential and commercial areas. It is often encountered in parks, along highways, and in backyards throughout its native region. The coastal bearded dragon, while not the species of bearded dragon to which this book is dedicated, is so similar to *P. vitticeps* in size, habit, diet, etc., that caring for one in captivity is virtually the same as caring for a true *P. vitticeps.* So similar, in fact, are these two species, that you might purchase a coastal bearded dragon (thinking it was an inland beardie), house it successfully for years, and never even know the difference! The only variable in housing these two species is that the coastal beardie, depending on the exact geographic location to which it was native, might require slightly higher levels of relative humidity. Some keepers have reported that they are more cold-tolerant than inland beardies, as well.

Pogona henrylawsoni

Another highly attractive species is the Lawson's dragon, *Pogona henrylawsoni*, which sports sandy and khaki hues that are typically much lighter in coloration than most other bearded dragons. Curiously enough, the Lawson's bearded dragon has virtually no "beard" to speak of. The Lawson's dragon is one of the smaller members of the *Pogona* clan, and large adults seldom exceed 10 to 11 inches (25.4 to 27.9 cm) in total length. Hailing from the sandy flat lands and scrub hillsides of central Queensland and the outskirts of the Northern Territory, the Lawson's Dragon is a diurnal omnivore who relies on its keen eyesight and fleetness of foot to both run down and capture prey, as well as to avoid being eaten itself. Because Lawson's dragon is the second most popular bearded dragon in the pet trade, the species is the subject of Chapter 8.

SVL

One measurement used often in herpetology is the snout-to-vent length, or SVL. This is the length of an animal measured from the tip of the nose across the belly to the cloaca, or vent. It excludes the tail. The reason the tail is excluded is that so many lizards (and to a lesser extent snakes and salamanders) lose their tails that including the tail length often gives an inaccurate impression of the animal's true size and, possibly, age.

Pogona microlepidota

Third in the genus is the Drysdale River bearded dragon, *P. microlepidota*. Growing to an average maximum body length of 4.5 to 5.5 inches (11.4 to 14 cm), this small beardie is native only to a tiny region of land in northwestern Australia immediately surrounding the Drysdale River basin. Because of this restricted range (and the fact that the scientific community knows less about this species than any other beardie), the Australian government places very strict protective regulations on the Drysdale River dragon (as well as all other indigenous wildlife), so encountering one on the legal pet trade is not very likely. Fond of basking atop fallen trees and in the tops of dense bushes, this fast, relatively slender dragon eats much more insect matter than do its larger cousins; insects may in fact comprise over 85 percent of its diet throughout its entire life. Because these species are so rarely encountered outside their natural range, many herp enthusiasts travel annually to the Drysdale River area hoping to catch a glimpse of one streaking across the highway or basking atop a stone.

The western bearded dragon is a small species that is almost never commercially available.

Pogona minima

The western bearded dragon, P. *minima*, is another small, slender member of the clan, but since its maximum snout-to-vent length does exceed 6 to 7 inches (15.2 to 17.8 cm), the western bearded dragon is considerably larger than the Drysdale River dragon. As its common name suggests, this dragon ranges widely across the extreme western and southwestern reaches of Australia. Do not confuse this species with the dwarf bearded dragon, however. Though the two are very similar at first glance, the western dragon displays a row of nuchal (back of the neck or nape) spines on either side of the head; these scale rows are absent in the dwarf dragon. Opportunistic feeders, the western beardies—with their fleetness of foot and sharp eyesight—are highly adapted for chasing down and catching insect prey. Juicy flowers, flower buds, and other succulent vegetation are also taken with relish. Like the Drysdale River dragon, the western bearded dragon is very rarely exported, thus any specimen you see for sale may well have been illegally collected. Check and double-check your source before purchasing such an animal, as no hobbyist among us wants to support the illegal collection of wildlife.

Pogona minor

Weighing in at approximately the same size as the western dragon, the dwarf bearded dragon, P. *minor*, ranges widely from the western Australian coast to deep within the continent's interior. Growing to an SVL of 6 to 7.5 inches (15.2 to 19.5 cm), the dwarf dragon is a species adapted to life in a variety of habitats, and may be found in woodlands, scrublands, rocky hillsides, deserts, rolling grasslands, and virtually any other habitat within its enormous geographic range. Like the previously mentioned bearded dragons, this species is a swift-moving omnivore whose diet consists of invertebrate prey, flowers, and other tender foliage. Despite this lizard's infrequent appearance in the wild, it is not rare. It is, rather, quite common; it's simply so skilled at staying hidden from sight that few people ever encounter one in the wild.

Pogona mitchelli

Mitchell's bearded dragon, *P. mitchelli*, is one of the smallest of the dragons. Its SVL rarely exceeds 5 to 6 inches (12.7 to 15.2 cm). Found throughout central and western Australia, the Mitchell's bearded dragon shares most of its range with the dwarf dragon. In areas where their ranges overlap, some experts suspect that the two species may interbreed, though more research is required to determine the truth behind this

Inland bearded dragons occur in a wide range of habitats, including woodlands, scrublands, and deserts.

Think Before Buying

Bearded dragons, like all herps, are not animals that should be purchased on a whim. They have special needs that must be met if they are to thrive in captivity. They are, however, easy to care for and hardy, so they make an excellent choice for the novice or beginning hobbyist, provided that hobbyist is willing to meet their needs.

Life Span

In the wild, bearded dragons may live for 3 to 6 years, with older specimens occurring only rarely. This short life span is due primarily to predation; bearded dragons appear on the menu of a great many Australian predators. In captivity, however, these lizards may thrive for up to 10 to 12 years if given superior care and proper nutrition through the years.

supposition. More research regarding Mitchell's bearded dragon is necessary to determine a great many things about this lizard, considering it was only described as a species 30 years ago. Although it closely resembles the dwarf bearded dragon, the Mitchell's dragon (like the western species) is distinguishable by the contiguous row of conical spines along the jaws and head. This omnivorous species fares quite well in captivity if provided with a spacious semi-arid enclosure and plenty of climbing branches.

Pogona nullarbor

If there were ever a beauty pageant among the beardies, the hands-down winner would be the banded bearded dragon, P. nullarbor. Also known as the Nullarbor Plains dragon, the banded bearded dragon is a small dragon, seldom exceeding 5 to 6 inches snout-to-vent length (12.7 to 15.2 cm). This species is the most strongly patterned of the dragons, wearing a dazzling coat of ivory bands evenly striped across the body beginning at the nape of the neck and extending well into the tail. Found only in a limited range in the Nullarbor Plains region of extreme south-central Australia, the banded bearded dragon thrives throughout eucalyptus groves, coastal forests, and sand flats. Though not overly common in the U.S. and European pet trade, this species would almost certainly boom in popularity among amateur and professional hobbyists alike if it were to hit the market in any numbers. Not only is the banded bearded dragon infinitely attractive, but it is also a hearty feeder in captivity, and it displays all the benign behaviors and irresistible charms of the popular inland bearded dragon.

Pogona vitticeps

The inland bearded dragon, P. vitticeps, is the animal to which this book is primarily dedicated. The "true" bearded dragon, this species is abundant in the pet trade. It frequently attains snout-to-vent length of 7 to 8 inches (17.8 to 20.3 cm), with a tail that comprises most of the overall body length—up to 22 inches (55.9 cm). Native to the east-central portion of Australia, the inland bearded dragon thrives both in the deep interior of the Outback, as well as on the fringes of human cities near the continent's south-central coast.

P. vitticeps dwells in a wide range of habitats including arid and semi-arid flatlands, deserts, forests, and grassy or rock-strewn hillsides. In developed areas, such as neighborhoods and farms, it's no rare thing to spot one of these dragons perched atop a fence rail, clinging to a shed or barn wall, basking in a driveway, or sunning along the edges of a parking lot. Despite their being considerably shorter than their coastal beardie cousins, the inland dragons are the most heavy-bodied of all the dragons. It should be noted, however, that captive specimens typically grow to much larger dimensions than their wild, free-ranging counterparts. This is due primarily to lack of exercise and excellent nutrition that the dragons receive in the captive environment.

Opportunistic omnivores, inland beardies will feed on just about any small animal or succulent vegetation they come across. Juveniles favor tiny insects, spiders, ants, etc., while adults will also take small vertebrates such as rodents, lizards, and some small snakes. Inland dragons take less and less animal fare as they mature; an adult diet may be composed of nearly 70 percent vegetable matter.

The beardies described above are as they occur in the wild. Decades of selective breeding and captive propagation have yielded some specialized dragons that would not be encountered in the wild. Larger dragons (i.e., the "German Giants"), more colorful dragons, and unusual hybrid dragons have all resulted from captive breeding projects, so there are a far greater variety of inland dragons available through the pet trade than you could ever encounter in the wilds of Australia.

Pet Dragons

What is it about the bearded dragons that make them so endearing and lovable to hobbyists? They have a number of interesting and charming traits that have earned them their popularity. Aside from ease of care, the two aspects of beardies that most win the heart of the hobbyist are the morphology, or appearance, and their behavior.

Smart Dragons

Bearded dragons are intelligent animals, and in captivity, they will soon learn to recognize their keeper. When you enter the room, do not be surprised if you see your dragon come charging to the front of its terrarium, just begging to be taken out, handled, and fed. They have even been known to learn what the cricket container or other food storage box looks like and become very excited when they see it.

Bearded dragons have a fringe of scales on their eyelids that may serve the same function as eyelashes in humans.

Morphology

Taking their common name from the "beard" of spiky scales lining the underside of their lower jaws, bearded dragons look like holdovers from the time of the dinosaurs. During the mating season, a male dragon's beard may turn gray, black, or even a dark blue, and he will puff it out to declare his intentions or ward off rival males.

A dragon's entire upper body (head, dorsum, flanks, etc.) is heavily scaled in tiny, spiky and conical scales, giving it a very rough, rugged appearance. Of course, if you've ever handled a beardie, you know that nothing could be further from the truth. These lizards are soft and pleasant to the touch; their "spiky" scales are really just for show, and their velvety belly is similarly soft. When basking in the sun, a dragon will raise the front half of its body high above its perch, leaving its back legs sprawled behind it. With head lifted and eyes wide and alert, the dragon (which has remarkably good eyesight for a reptile and can see for a considerable distance) looks statuesque—like a cold-blooded sentinel on watch for danger. When a hobbyist enters the room, an alert and keen-eyed beardie will quickly spot him or her, and it may charge forward, begging to be taken out and played with or fed.

Behaviors

Not only are dragons adored for their physical appearance, but they are also prized for the unique behaviors they display in captivity, which many hobbyists find cute or even comical.

Arm Waving Hatchling and baby beardies are renowned for their arm-waving practices. Sitting on the substrate or basking atop a stone, a baby beardie will, for no apparent reason, raise one of its forelimbs off the ground, hold its claw above its head, and slowly and in a jerky fashion, lower it back to the substrate. Sometimes, they will wave their arm in circles

Normally colored bearded dragons have a dark black spot right above the shoulders. If this spot has a function in nature, it is not currently known.

before lowering it. On the surface level, it appears that your tiny pet might be stretching or even waving "Hello" to you. In the wild, bearded dragons are semi-social animals that exhibit low-level forms of communication with others of their species. Juveniles and females may wave their arms as a sign of being submissive or non-threatening to other nearby dragons.

Head Bobbing

The opposite gesture of the arm-wave is the head-bob. When a dragon rapidly bobs its head, it is sending a challenge or warning to any nearby dragons. If, for example, one dragon is sitting atop a desirable perch and another dragon wishes to take it, the intruder will rapidly bob his head to issue the challenge. If he does not want to give up the perch, the resident male will respond aggressively by rapidly bobbing his head, and, although it is rare among inland bearded dragons, territorial combat may ensue. Such dominant/submissive gestures and behaviors are not uncommon in the reptile world, and are especially prevalent in iguanid and agamid lizards, as well as in alligators and crocodiles.

When a resident male bobs his head while facing a much smaller male, the opposite scenario will occur. Once the larger male has given his head-bobbing challenge, the smaller male will respond by waving his arms and giving the sign that he wants no trouble. Similar events occur during the mating season. When a male wishes to mate with a female, he'll bob his head and wait. If she responds by waving her arms, then he has the green light to approach and mate, although most adult male dragons will attempt to breed with a female even if she is hesitant or resistant. These behaviors are exhibited both in the wild and in captivity when multiple dragons are housed together.

Stacking Speaking of multiple housing, a curious thing often occurs when more than one dragon is housed in the same enclosure. Through a practice known as stacking, captive dragons will perch one atop the other in order to bask in the warmest, brightest part of the terrarium. While stacking may be a cute behavior, it is best that each individual animal be given plenty of basking space to call its own, for the dragons on the bottom of the stack will not receive the same degree of beneficial ultraviolet radiation as does the dragon on top. Additionally, the breathing of the dragon on the bottom of the stack may be somewhat impaired. A great many

Bearded dragons may pile on top of one another at a desirable basking spot.

photos exist of size-stacked dragons, with the adult on the bottom, the subadult in the middle, and the baby on the top. Again, this may make for a charming scene, but animals of multiple sizes should never be housed together, as the smaller individuals will likely be bullied or injured.

Billowing Beard Perhaps the most famous of all beardie displays, however, is the billowing beard. When a dragon is confronted by a predator or other threat, it will hold its mouth agape, puff up its beard of prickly scales, and hiss at its would-be attacker, all the while raising its head and fore-portions off the ground in a threatening display. The beard swells to many times its normal size, darkens very quickly to a black or burnished blue color, and gives the predator the illusion that the largely defenseless bearded dragon is a scary, feisty, monstrosity of a lizard and that coming one step closer would be a bad idea! This is the bearded dragon's best illusion, for aside from its powerful jaws and mildly serrate teeth, a bearded dragon would make a plump, juicy meal for a hungry predator. Merely because the dragon can look ferocious doesn't mean that it is, but most predators don't know that. When rival males meet in the wild, each will also billow out its beard in an attempt to intimidate the other. When this works, territorial disputes are solved without the lizards resorting to combat. In captivity, most bearded dragons quickly abandon this natural survival tool, and may live their entire lives without ever flaring their beards in aggression or defense.

When a bearded dragon feels threatened or meets a potential rival, it will puff out and darken its beard to appear larger and more menacing.

Chapter 2

Acquiring a Healthy Dragon

Once you've decided that a bearded dragon is the lizard for you, you must take all necessary steps to ensure that the dragon you select is in peak health. Purchasing a sickly or otherwise inferior dragon will most likely result in a short, problematic, and ultimately depressing endeavor that ends with a dead dragon and a herp-wary hobbyist. Getting it right from day one is the first step in ensuring a long, healthy, and happy life for your dragon. Of course, there are various sources through which you may acquire your dragon, and there are guidelines to follow when purchasing from each of these sources. Prerequisite to making a purchase from any source, however, is the construction of the dragon's habitat. It is a cardinal sin of any herp endeavor to purchase the animal without having previously built a warm and secure habitat that is waiting at home to receive the new dragon.

Pet Stores

Ah, the pet shop. The old standby, a friendly neighborhood pet shop overflowing with fish tanks, squawking parrots, and exotic reptiles of all sorts. Most potential beardie owners first encounter these delightful reptiles in a local pet shop.

The Shop Itself

The first thing to look for when surveying bearded dragons (either babies or adults) in the pet shop is the cleanliness of the shop and of the terrarium in which the dragons are housed. Is the terrarium clean and brightly lit? Is it decorated with hiding places and climbing materials? Or is the floor of the tank littered with feces, overturned water dishes, and other such filth? Are a great number of dragons crammed together in an inadequately small terrarium?

If the terrarium in which the dragons are housed is disgusting and dirty, it is highly likely that the dragons will be in poor health. Parasites, bacteria, and fungi all

Most of the bearded dragons offered for sale at pet stores will be hatchlings or juveniles less than six months old.

Careful Handling

When you handle a prospective pet beardie at the pet shop, make sure you hold it over a counter or table, preferably with a soft towel or cloth lying under it. Baby bearded dragons may appear calm and slow moving, but if startled, they can move with surprising speed and can easily leap from a handler's hands without warning. Therefore, make sure the little dragon will neither fall far when he leaps nor land on a hard surface, as such impact can seriously injure the frail baby dragon.

thrive under rancid conditions, so any dragons housed in filth are definitely not purchase-worthy. Similarly, dragons that are housed too densely (more than 5 hatchlings in a 10-gallon [37.9 l] terrarium) are subject to stress and stress-related maladies. I personally recommend against purchasing an individual from a densely stocked terrarium of dragons.

The Dragons

Once you've found a terrarium of dragons that is clean and well maintained, you'll want to visually study the dragons themselves. Healthy baby bearded dragons are alert animals, but they are also mild-mannered. Most baby lizards (geckos, anoles, iguanas, etc.) will flee when you approach the terrarium, but beardies, owing to their individual personalities, may react in any number of ways. The most high-strung dragons may take cover or hide at your approach; the average dragons may eye you suspiciously and ready themselves for flight should your hand enter the cage; and some of the most personable baby dragons will crawl toward you, nosing at the glass and studying you just as hard as you are studying them! Dragons with this type of personality as hatchlings have the greatest chance of becoming "dog tame," meaning that the lizard will act toward you with the same benevolent curiosity as a puppy.

Don't Buy a Sick Dragon

It may be highly tempting to buy an obviously sick bearded dragon in hopes of saving it, but don't do it. Purchasing a sick beardie in order to rehabilitate it almost always ends with a dead lizard, a smaller bank account, and your heart broken. It is difficult to rehabilitate a sick reptile, even for veterinarians and wildlife rehabilitators. Additionally, by purchasing a sick beardie, you have financially rewarded a vendor for mistreating his or her animals. It is better to pass on the dragon (that will most likely die whether you buy it or not), inform the vendor that the dragon is sick, and take your business elsewhere.

Whatever the personality type of the baby dragons in question, they should do *something* at your approach; they should be aware of your presence and react in some way, even if it is a seemingly insignificant reaction. Even the baby dragons that do not take immediate note of your presence should be behaving in a normal fashion: basking on a limb, eating, crawling about, etc. Take any limp, lethargic, or otherwise lifeless dragons as a red flag that something is seriously wrong, and know that such dragons are likely in a dire state of health. Do not purchase such dragons.

The next step is to reach into the terrarium and remove a baby dragon. Again, owing to their mild dispositions, baby beardies may not always take to immediate flight, though most will retreat from your hand. Grasp the baby dragon gently if you must pick it up outright, though the preferred method is to lay your hand flat in the tank, palm up. With your other hand, gently corral the baby dragon into your waiting palm. Close your fingers gently around the dragon and lift it from the tank. Some babies will sit quietly in your palm or look about curiously. A healthy baby dragon will continually look around and will likely walk all over your hand, lowering its head and lightly licking your fingers and hand. This tasting behavior is natural and is a crucial sign that the animal is curious, alert, and healthy. A dragon that feels limp, doesn't move, rests with its eyes closed, or doesn't seem otherwise alert when picked up is a suffering dragon (it may have an internal injury or parasite load resulting from filthy conditions in transport) and will not likely live much longer.

This time you spend handling the baby dragon is also an excellent opportunity to inspect the animal physically. Does the dragon have any cuts, sores, or open lesions? Are all the toes and tip of the tail present, and if not, are the stumps healed without any signs of infection? Does the dragon seem to have adequate weight for its size? This last question may be difficult for the new hobbyist to answer, as baby beardies are tiny animals that seem to have the weight of a feather. Inspect the dragon's eyes: Are they open, clear, and alert, or are they closed, crusty, or runny? Inspect also the animal's cloaca. Is it closed and free of any clinging debris? It is important that all the dragon's bodily openings be healthy and functioning

Even hatchling dragons as defensive as these will usually settle down and become tame pets.

Signs of an Unhealthy Dragon

The list below contains the signs of an unhealthy or otherwise unsuitable dragon. Check this list against the dragon you are thinking of purchasing.

- The dragon is listless, limp, or otherwise inactive and uninterested in its environment.
- The dragon keeps his eyes closed, or the eyes appear sunken.
- There is crust or exudate around the eyes, nostrils, or vent.
- Any of the limbs appear broken, misshapen, or useless.
- The jaws are soft or misshapen.
- There is cheesy yellow matter in the mouth.
- The dragon has unhealed wounds or burns.

It is okay if the prospective purchase is missing toes or the tip of the tail, as long as the stumps are completely healed and do not seem to hinder the dragon's movements.

properly. Inspect the dragon's limbs for any signs of breaks or fractures. Baby dragons are quite fragile, and broken limbs can and do occur during the rigors of transport and shipping. Any limbs that appear swollen, discolored, or lame may well be injured.

Other Considerations

Well, if you've found a baby bearded dragon that passes all these tests, you've likely found a fine pet. A final consideration before making a purchase rests with the pet shop itself. Does the pet shop have a resident reptile expert who can answer any questions and solve any problems that might arise in the keeping of a bearded dragon? You might be surprised just how helpful a knowledgeable expert can be in a time of crisis. If the shop is poorly staffed, or if the clerks don't seem to know about their beardies, you might consider searching for a more professional pet shop. Once you've satisfied all the requirements listed here, it's time to make your purchase and take your bearded dragon home.

Internet Vendors

With the advent of the Internet, traders, sellers, and merchants can now make their wares available to a worldwide market. Professional breeders of bearded dragons are no exception.

A slightly older dragon will be larger and hardier than a hatchling. Compare the size difference between this four-month old and this two-month old.

Professional and amateur breeders from all over the globe now offer their stock online. The foremost advantage to purchasing from an online professional breeder is the peace of mind and quality assurance offered by the breeder. Because professional breeders stake their livelihoods on their sales, they often will go above and beyond the call of duty in ensuring that you, the customer, receive the best and healthiest lizard available. Unlike the pet shop purchase, the online professional breeder purchase will virtually guarantee that you are purchasing a healthy lizard, which is cataloged in the breeder's database and which comes with all paperwork, including hatch date, feeding regimen, growth rate, etc.

Likewise, professional breeders are profoundly knowledgeable about bearded dragons, and most of them will never hesitate to answer emails, phone calls, or letters you send in regard to any questions or problems that might arise with your dragon. In short, professional breeders take each and every dragon seriously and will be a lifelong resource and friend to the customer who stays in touch. All this quality assurance and customer care does not come cheap, however, and the hobbyist should be aware that a premium bearded dragon will cost a premium price. But, most serious hobbyists agree that having a happy, healthy, and long-term relationship with their dragons is well worth the initial investment price of purchasing from a professional breeder.

The drawback to the online purchase is that you do not get to physically inspect the animal before making a purchase. In the case of professionally raised dragons, this is a small matter, as the breeder will provide a superior animal regardless. When purchasing from a forum or herp classified ad website, however, this lack of physical inspection can be problematic.

When purchasing from a non-professional breeder online, you'll typically only have a few photos of the animal in question and a short written description about the dragon. Send a few emails to the seller before you commit to purchase. Ask the seller everything you can about the health of the dragon (make a checklist of the features described here: cleanliness of environment, attitude, physical state, dietary regimen, etc.). If you happen upon a seller who seems reluctant to answer your questions or to send you any additional photos of the animal in question, take this as a red flag that you are dealing with a sub-par seller, and you should probably look to trade elsewhere.

Doing a little research on the retailer or seller in which you are interested never hurts. Find out what other buyers have to say about that seller. This research can save you a lot of time, money, and heartache, as a great many shiftless, cunning online sellers may call themselves professional breeders, when in fact these people have only their financial interests in mind and may send you a lizard of inferior quality. Do your homework to avoid getting burned. There are several online forums that discuss sales experience with herp vendors.

Herp Shows

If you're a reptile or amphibian hobbyist who has never been to a herp show, shame on you! Seriously though, herp shows, or reptile expos as they are sometimes called, are events in which dozens, hundreds, or even thousands of vendors—wholesalers, importers, professional breeders, and hobby breeders—put their reptile and amphibian livestock on display for sale to the public. Usually held at farmer's markets, coliseums, lecture halls, or other large public gathering places, these shows allow the hobbyist to browse through an almost limitless variety of reptiles and amphibians. The penny-wise herper can find more than a few bargains at such shows.

Because bearded dragons are so popular, it is almost guaranteed that several vendors will have a large selection of bouncing baby beardies, and it is also a guarantee that these vendors will be trying to undersell one another to attract more customers.

Herp Classifieds

Most herp-specific magazines have classified sections in the back of them and breeder advertisements throughout. These ads often are taken out by professional breeders who wish to advertise their stock somewhere other than the Internet, and most offer high-quality stock at reasonable prices. As is true of all long distance purchases, however, do some research on the seller to make certain of their credentials and their commitment to quality dragons and customer care.

The benefits of attending a herp show are many. They include the variety of stock, generally low prices, and possible good end-of-the-show deals, and the time you want to physically inspect and handle any individual dragon is mostly unconstrained.

Of course, like all other forms of beardie purchase, the reptile expo is not without its drawbacks. The first of these disadvantages is that, for the most part, all purchases are final. Virtually no herp show vendor will offer refunds or exchanges on their herps. These shows are a sort of liquidation frenzy among vendors, so don't expect a liberal refund policy. Second, once you've bought a dragon, you're on your own. The pet shop clerk and the online professional breeder will both be there to answer your questions and help to solve any dragon-related problems, but once the show ends, the vendors pack up and disappear. You can occasionally catch a vendor who is interested in building a reputation as a professional breeder, or you might buy from a renowned breeder who has set up shop at the expo. These sellers will give you a business card and may be of future help, but these sellers are in the minority. The odds are that after you make purchase, you'll never see your vendor again. Consider all swaps, trades, and purchases final.

Buying an Adult

Most hobbyists will purchase a baby dragon because the growth and development of these lizards from one stage of life to the next is a great part of the fun of owning one. Hobbyists all want to see their scaly, little friends feed and grow up. But the purchasing of an adult beardie is certainly not out of the question.

Adult dragons can make excellent pets, as they are already grown and the most delicate phase of life is behind them. While most adult dragons will command considerably higher prices than their younger counterparts, some professional breeders will sell their older breeding stock at reduced prices. Old females that have produced several broods of young may be sold at reasonable prices, as

You may want to consider starting with adult dragons, which are sometimes available from breeders for reasonable prices.

the breeder's resources are limited and he or she cannot always dedicate space and food supplies to non-breeding animals. If you're in the market for a mature dragon, one of these old gals might be just the thing for you.

Remember that all the same rules of inspection and physical hygiene and health that apply to babies also apply to adult dragons. Purchasing an adult dragon all but guarantees a shorter life span for the lizard and a shorter keeper/pet relationship for both of you. Since the average life span of a healthy dragon in captivity is 9 to 12 years, the purchase of a 6-year-old dragon leaves you with a maximum of 6 more years with your pet, while the purchase of a healthy baby can leave you with over a decade of beardie bliss.

A final consideration in the purchase of a bearded dragon is the matter of a veterinarian. Once a rarity, herp vets are becoming more and more common as the demand for their skills increases. Not only will a herp vet help you protect your investment — and the purchase of a premium dragon, its terrarium, habitat, etc. can be a real investment — but he or she will also curb illness, fight infection, heal wounds, and diagnose and treat any number of maladies that could strike your dragon. I once heard that you should find a good herp vet before you find a good herp, and I couldn't agree more. With a good herp vet in your corner, you and your dragon stand a much better chance for a long, healthy, and happy relationship.

Adoption

It is a sad fact that many owners of bearded dragons do not keep them throughout their entire life span. Generally, this happens because they were unprepared for costs in time and money that caring for a dragon entails. Additionally, people move, divorce, grow up, change jobs, go to college, and have other life changes that can render them unable to provide for a beardie. While many of these people sell their dragons or give them to a willing friend, others give their dragons up for adoption. Dragons do show up at animal shelters, which are usually not prepared to care for a heat-loving omnivorous lizard.

If you want an adult dragon, or want to help save a bearded dragon from its orphaned state, adopting someone's former pet may be for you. Check your local animal shelter periodically to see if a beardie shows up. You can call and ask that they keep you in mind should one be surrendered to the shelter. There are also herp-only adoption services. Some of these are listed in the back of this book.

Chapter 3

Housing and Habitats

When it comes to housing your bearded dragon, there is a cardinal rule that must never be broken: Fully construct your beardie's terrarium before you purchase the dragon. Transport from the pet shop (or shipping direct from the breeder) is a stressful time for your dragon, and the longer you keep it sitting around waiting in a cold, dark box while you build its habitat, the more likely your dragon is to stress and take ill. A smooth, swift transition from the pet shop to a warm terrarium in your home is the first and foremost step in minimizing the stress of transit.

Keep Strict Quarantine

If you own other herps, you should do your utmost to keep the new dragon in quarantine truly separated from your healthy, established pets. The quarantine tank should be set up in a different room from your other herps. Always feed, clean, and otherwise service the quarantine tank after performing your duties to the established herps first. This prevents contaminating your healthy pets, in the event the new dragon should have some communicable illness.

Quarantine

The conscientious herp hobbyist will construct for his or her incoming beardie a quarantine tank, which, in times of future trouble or illness, will double as a hospital tank. The quarantine tank is a place where all the lizard's basic needs are met, but where the hobbyist will be able to carefully observe the animal for any signs of illness, parasites, distress, etc. To accommodate maximum viewing efficiency, outfit the quarantine terrarium sparsely and with minimal clutter. A dark hide box, white paper-towel substrate, an artificial climb, and a small water dish are all that you need.

House and feed your dragon normally while it is in quarantine, though I do not recommend offering food for 8-12 hours after bringing it home from the pet shop. Allow your dragon this much time to adapt to the sights and sounds of its new surroundings. Maintain proper temperatures and lighting regimens in the quarantine tank. If, after two weeks of close monitoring, you can find no signs of illness or dismay in your dragon, you may transfer the newly arrived lizard into its permanent terrarium.

The quarantine period is especially critical if you keep multiple dragons or a collection of various types of reptiles and amphibians. Should you bring an infected beardie directly into contact with your other herps (by direct contact, I mean in the same enclosure, or even into the same room of your house as the rest of your herps), you risk infecting your entire collection. Avoid compromising the safety and health of your herps by maintaining your quarantine area in a room on the opposite side of your house from the rest of your collection. All fixtures, water dishes, light bulbs, etc. that are used in quarantine must never be moved to the general housing area. Minimize the risk of contamination by keeping the quarantine terrarium and all associated equipment well away from the rest of your herps.

Glass aquaria are the most frequently used housing for bearded dragons, but there are other suitable options.

The Enclosure
Size

The first aspect of the permanent "home" terrarium to be considered is its size. While a 20-gallon "long" tank (76 l)—30 inches long x 12 inches wide x 10 inches high (76. 2 cm x 30.5 cm x 25.4 cm)—will provide ample living space for a baby beardie, you must remember that healthy dragons grow quickly. In less than a year's time, this size cage will be horribly cramped for your sub-adult dragon. Bearded dragons are naturally active animals, and even small individuals require spacious enclosures with ample room to move about.

A good, long-term terrarium size is the standard 125 gallon tank (473 l)—72" L x 18" W x 16"H (183 cm x 45.7 cm x 40.6 cm)—which will provide ample living space for even the largest adult dragon throughout its entire life. Take note how this space is distributed throughout the terrarium, however, as the bearded dragon has needs that are very different from some other types of herps. The barrel-bellied bearded dragons require plenty of horizontal space—floor space—in which to roam. For this reason, tanks with broad stretches of floor space are much preferred over taller, narrower terrariums. So the absolute floor space of the terrarium is more important than the absolute volume.

Type

A second question that often arises when housing bearded dragons is what kind of enclosure you should use. Glass aquariums, such as those designed to house fish, are excellent choices. They are easily cleaned, provide excellent visibility for viewing pleasure (both yours looking in and your dragon's looking out), and, barring a serious accident, these tanks will last a very long time.

Plastic or acrylic terrariums have recently become popular among reptile hobbyists, as they are lightweight, easy to maintain (i.e., sliding front doors allow for quick and easy cleaning), they hold heat very well, and they are aesthetically pleasing inside the home. While these enclosures are well suited for a range of snakes, I cannot recommend them for bearded dragons. Acrylics and plastics are easily scratched, and, as bearded dragons are often housed on a sandy substrate, the acrylic tank can quickly take on a frosted, sandblasted appearance, thereby reducing visibility into the dragon's habitat and transforming an otherwise beautiful terrarium into something of an eyesore. Some come with glass doors, and these would be more acceptable. Another drawback to acrylic terrariums is that they may not allow for as much ventilation as your dragon will require. Acrylic tanks are renowned for holding in moisture and humidity (making them perfect for tropical boids and amphibians), both of which are definitely detrimental to the health and long-term welfare of the desert-going bearded dragon.

Some breeders and owners of large collections use cattle watering troughs to house their beardies.

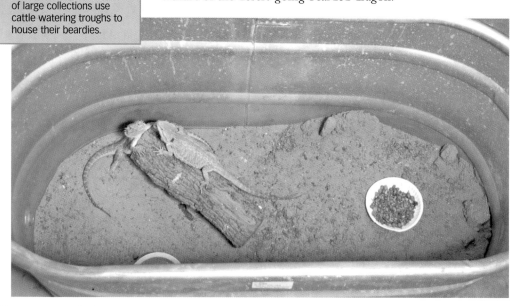

Serious breeders or other hobbyists who are not concerned with aesthetics may also employ large cattle or horse water troughs as housing for their dragons. Troughs provide plenty of floor space, and they can easily be heated/illuminated by attaching a clamp-lamp to the rim and angling its rays into the trough. While a great many breeders use troughs for both living quarters and egg-laying habitats, their opaque metal sides do not allow the dragon to see beyond its enclosure in any direction. Like being trapped in a great hole in the ground, the beardie is forced to stare at bland, metal walls everyday. Bearded dragons are intelligent animals whose eyesight is quite good for a lizard. I believe, therefore, that in the long-term, the lack of visual stimulation is a detriment to the mental health, stress level, appetite, and, eventually, the immune system of beardies housed in troughs. This lack of stimulation can, however, be counteracted if the hobbyist takes his or her dragon out of the trough and handles and exercises it daily. Additionally, if you are housing several dragons in a trough, they will have each other to interact with.

Security

Security in the bearded dragon enclosure is an important matter, but it is also one that hinges largely on the conditions under which each individual dragon is housed. If housed in a horse trough or in a deep, open-topped terrarium, the likelihood of escape on the part of the dragon is minimal, just so long as the lizard cannot scale any high stones or tall basking branches and crawl out and over the sides of the enclosure. Keeping an open top on such an enclosure is beneficial to the humidity and air flow within the enclosure.

If, however, you have tall climbing perches or a shorter terrarium, then you'll need to secure the terrarium. Most commercially made terraria and fish tanks have lids that are specially sized to fit snugly. Lids that have heavy metal screen and a metal frame are the best. Lids that have a plastic frame will almost certainly warp, melt, or burn under the intense light and heat that you must supply to your dragon. Metal lids do not suffer from this problem.

If a heavy gauge screen lid is enough to keep your dragon in, is it enough to keep any unwanted visitors out? When the family cat comes prowling around the terrarium, you'll want to have a locking lid fitted tightly to the terrarium to prevent your dragon from ending up as a kitty treat and to keep an adult dragon from nipping the nose of your beloved feline. Similarly, any unsupervised children can easily be kept at bay with a locking lid. When a young child handles a dragon unsupervised, both the child and the dragon are at risk. The child may run a health risk by putting his or her hands in their mouth or even putting part of the dragon in their mouth, and the dragon is at risk of bodily injury under the sometimes raucous and excitable hands of a child. A secure terrarium with a tight, locking lid will keep all parties safe and happy.

Humidity

Once you have decided on what style of housing you will employ for your dragon, you must approach the issue of humidity and ventilation. Beardies are desert lizards, and a low degree of relative humidity is vital to their survival in captivity. Avoid all glass or plastic terrarium lids, as these will cause the air inside the terrarium to stagnate and become problematic to your lizard's respiratory system. Lids made of heavy gauge mesh wire or rubberized screen mounted into a plastic or metal frame are the best. Not only do these lids allow for ample amounts of fresh oxygen to enter the terrarium, but they also provide for the dissipation of humidity and noxious gases associated with your dragon's respiration and defecation.

Humidity can also be kept in check by using only small water dishes in your dragon's terrarium, for excessively large water dishes will increase the humidity inside the terrarium as the water inside them evaporates. If you live in an excessively humid area, such as on the coast or in swampy lowlands, your dragons might require a dehumidifier to be placed in the room. Ideal relative humidity in the bearded dragon habitat is 35 to 40 percent, which is almost identical to the relative humidity that inland bearded dragons would encounter in the wilderness of Australia. Under normal captive circumstances, however, no additional equipment is necessary to maintain a sufficiently low relative humidity of 45 to 50 percent.

If the walls of the terrarium are high enough, you may not need a lid. However, in most cases a secure cage top will be necessary.

The only exception to this humidity rule is the coastal bearded dragon, *P. barbata*, which will do well with slightly higher humidity, although it should still not exceed 55 percent.

Substrate

When it comes to the matter of substrate in the terrarium, there is considerable and often contentious debate among hobbyists about which ones are best.

Sand and Similar Materials

In nature, the bearded dragon will spend its entire life atop the pebbles and fine sands of the Australian Outback. However, some hobbyists believe housing dragons on sand runs the risk of them suffering a gut impaction. An impacted gut occurs when the dragon ingests small quantities of sand and is unable to pass them. The dragon's intestinal tract then becomes blocked and causes a wide range of health problems, including death if not treated. In over 25 years of housing a wide range of desert reptiles on sand, I have never had a specimen suffer from an impacted gut.

Pebbles and gravel are often sold as suitable substrates for desert reptiles. However, one of my bearded dragons required surgery to remove intestinal blockage caused by tiny aquarium pebbles. Not only can aquarium gravel cause impaction, but a hungry beardie can easily damage its teeth and jaws when biting down on a pebble, should it grasp one along with a cricket or mealworm. Finally, wastes tend to sink down beneath the pebbles, creating an unhealthy bacterial breeding ground. Pebbles and gravel cannot be recommended as a substrate for bearded dragons.

If an impacted gut is a concern, but you still want to use a sandy substrate, you have two options. Your first choice is to employ smooth, non-silica sand as you would normally, then sprinkle a light dusting of calcium supplement over the surface of the sand, churn the supplement into the sand, then sprinkle the surface again. This dusting of the substrate ensures that if your dragon ingests any sand along with its meal, it will also ingest a small amount of calcium supplement, which will stimulate the dragon's digestive tract and help it to pass any ingested sand. As you change the dragon's substrate at cleaning time, you will need to reseed the sand with ample amounts of calcium powder.

Hazardous Carpet

Artificial turf and indoor/outdoor carpet are not recommended substrates for bearded dragon terraria. The tiny fibers from the carpet can become entangled around the toe tips of your dragon. Working their way under the scales, these fibers are virtually invisible and will constrict the blood flow to the toe. Over time, this will lead to the shriveling up and falling off of the toe. This microfiber amputation is also common among hobbyists who allow their pets to roam about on the carpeted floors of their homes. Another hazard posed by this type of substrate is that little bits of the plastic can break off and be swallowed by the dragon, possibly causing gut impactions, choking, and injuries.

A second option is to purchase a calcium-based sand at your local pet shop. There are several brands available. They are actually crafted from calcium, so any grains of this artificial sand that your dragon ingests will simply be metabolized or passed through the body with no ill effects. On the plus side, these manufactured sands prevent impacting and come in a wide variety of colors for the hobbyist who is concerned with aesthetics. The major

Sand is the substrate preferred by most bearded dragon keepers.

drawback to calcium sand is its exorbitant price. It will cost many times the price of regular sand. There is definitely a fiscal trade off between these two options.

If you do opt for a sandy substrate (either smooth, non-silica, or calcium-based), you'll need to layer it at least 3 to 4 inches (7.6 to 10.2 cm) deep over the floor of the terrarium. In the wild, bearded dragons naturally burrow for various reasons. Sometimes your beardie will bury nearly its entire body in the sand with only its head exposed for the purposes of thermoregulation or sleep. Nervous or stressed dragons (such as those specimens recently arriving from transit) may also find great comfort in burrowing beneath the substrate. Whatever the reason, burrowing is a big part of a bearded dragon's natural behavior. A very shallow layer of sand will greatly distress the dragon, for the shallowness of the sand will continually frustrate your dragon's digging attempts and can inflict much undue stress.

Cage Liners

Of course, sand isn't the only acceptable substrate for the bearded dragon enclosure. Hobbyists far and wide report success when housing a dragon atop commercially manufactured cage liners and reptile cage carpet—not to be confused with indoor/outdoor carpet or artificial turf. The major benefit of these carpets are the ease of cleaning. When the carpet becomes soiled, simply remove it from the terrarium and wash it in hot water with antibacterial soap, rinse thoroughly, and allow it to dry before replacing. The thinness of the reptile carpet also helps the dragon to soak up maximum amounts of heat from any undertank heating pads you might employ. A thin layer of substrate will buffer this heat, thereby minimizing any benefit the undertank heating pad might offer.

The sand sold for use in reptile enclosures is available in several colors.

Bark, Mulch, and Wood Shavings

Bark chips and garden mulch (there are a wide variety of these substrates available in most pet shops) can also be used, but you must remember that the bearded dragon is a desert-dweller. Moisture-retaining substrates such as mulches, barks, and soils may keep the terrarium too humid to accommodate a bearded dragon. Use caution when employing these substrates and make sure that the humidity inside the terrarium stays within acceptable limits. If you can control the humidity, they make acceptable substrates.

Pine and cedar chips, shavings, or any other evergreen products must *never be used* in the beardie terrarium. Pine and cedar contain heavily scented oils and resins that can permanently damage the olfactory organs (i.e., the nose, tongue, and sinuses), respiratory system, and the skin. Not only will your pet's ability to smell and taste be compromised, but these oils and resins will cause a great deal of stress to your dragon (remember that stress is a gateway ailment that easily leads to loss of appetite and a depressed immune system). I've seen individuals housed on odiferous cedar shavings that absolutely refused to feed. When removed to a more appropriate enclosure, however, those same individuals began feeding with much fervor.

Paper Products

Another type of bedding that you can use is the recycled newspaper. Literally manufactured from the washed and shredded remains of recycled newsprint, this bedding is fluffy, lightweight, and poses minimal threat to the dragon if a small bit of it is ingested. I personally never use newspaper bedding due to its propensity for trapping and holding in moisture. I live in Georgia, a state renowned for its high levels of relative humidity, and recycled newspaper bedding doesn't work well for maintaining the desert-like conditions the dragons need.

Recycled paper is a safe and effective bedding for bearded dragons.

In other parts of the country, however, or in a climate-controlled environment equipped with a dehumidifier, recycled newspaper could work very well. Animal wastes also soak deeply into recycled newsprint, as do the odors associated with them, making clean up a little more intense than in a sand mixture that clumps well around animal wastes. Recycled newspaper bedding is widely available at any pet retailer or via the Internet.

A large number of hobbyists also like to use plain old newspaper for bedding. It's cheap, and it's easily disposed of and replaced during clean-up. However, it is aesthetically unpleasant, and it denies your dragon the ability to burrow. Dragons have a natural fixation with burrowing (for purposes of sleeping at night, hiding from predators, thermoregulation, etc.), and they should be able to exercise this ability while under our care. Dragons housed on newspaper will often pull it up and squirm beneath it. Unfortunately, they will then often defecate under the newspaper, making a nasty mess.

Cage Furnishings
Wood and Branches

For starters, you'll want to invest in a solid, wide, tall climbing branch. Beardies absolutely love to climb, perch, and bask on an adequately sized climbing branch. For hatchling and juvenile specimens, a length of sandblasted grapevine works nicely. Available at any pet shop that deals in herp-related products, sandblasted grapevines are porous, gnarly, and work very well as climbs for smaller dragons. The vine's surface nature allows the minuscule lizards to easily climb, bask, and even sleep atop the vine should they desire.

Grapevine is typically too small to accommodate the girth and bulk of larger bearded dragons, so a larger climb will be necessary. Large hunks of cured driftwood (not painted or shellacked), especially those with flat, broad surfaces upon them, make excellent climbs for adult dragons. Both sandblasted grapevine and driftwood slabs can be washed, are long-lasting items, will simulate the sun-bleached

Eliminate the Undesirables

Before placing a stone into the bearded dragon terrarium, I always wrap it in aluminum foil and "bake" it in the oven for 30 minutes at 250°F (121.1°C). Most rocks have tiny pores that may hold bacteria, mold, spores, or even parasites that can cause harm to your dragon. Baking the stone ensures that these micro-creeps are destroyed utterly. Allow the rock to cool completely before placing it in your dragon's tank.

logs and fallen branches atop which your beardie would naturally bask in the wild, and are aesthetically pleasing when used in a naturalistic terrarium.

Rocks

Large rocks are also an option, as beardies are no less at home basking atop a stone as they are on a wooden perch. Quarries and stone masons will often give you a couple of stones for free if you simply ask. Garden shops and hardware/garden stores also sell stones, as do most pet shops. Sandstones are not only flat and hold heat well, but their bright orange and reddish hues are aesthetically pleasing in the display tank.

Of course, very large natural stones are also *very heavy* and can easily crack the glass floor of your terrarium. Artificial or ceramic stones are available at pet shops and in the garden section of most hardware stores; these rugged items make excellent substitutes for the real thing. Not only are artificial stones naturalistic in appearance, but they are also very lightweight. Some are hollow and may double as hides when your lizard wishes to retire.

Plants

Plants are also an option in the beardie terrarium, but the hobbyist must take care in what types of plants he or she selects. Artificial plants are probably your best option, as they need no water, do not shed leaves, never die, and are easily removed, washed, and returned to the terrarium at cleaning time. A good stand of either plastic or silk vegetation can add a definite degree of aesthetic beauty and naturalistic cover for your dragon, while at the same time requiring minimal upkeep and maintenance on your part.

Bearded dragons at every stage of life enjoy climbing rocks and branches, so provide some in your enclosure.

Living plants, on the other hand, can present a wide range of difficulties in the home terrarium. Living plants require frequent watering that may saturate the terrarium's substrate. During photosynthesis, they emit water vapor into the air, so any species of living plant you use will significantly raise the relative humidity in your dragon's enclosure.

Because of the omnivorous nature of your dragon, you may also encounter other problems when using live plants in that your beardie may see a great many terrarium plants as food and may nibble on them. While they may appear tasty to your dragon, some species of plant may possess toxins or resins that can pose serious risks to your lizard should it munch on them. Even if the species of plant you choose contain no harmful chemicals or resins, you are still faced with the constant problem of the dragon eating the décor of its terrarium. Adult dragons can break over all but the most stalwart and sturdy of terrarium plants. The long and the short of it is that unless you are constructing a very specialized living vivarium, live plants can be much more of a burden than they are worth in the bearded dragon terrarium.

If you simply must have some type of live plant in your bearded dragon's enclosure, however, several varieties of juniper are recommended. The slow-growing, woody stemmed junipers, which require small amounts of water and which emit minimal amounts of water vapor, are by far the most long-lasting and aesthetically pleasing plants you could ever place in your dragon's enclosure. For ease of cleaning and maintenance, it is best to pot the juniper shrub in a shallow clay or terra-cotta pot. Then bury the pot up to the rim in the sandy substrate of your dragon's enclosure. This makes for a very aesthetically pleasing and naturalistic terrarium, while at the same time allowing for extreme ease in cleaning—simply remove the potted juniper, change the terrarium substrate, and rebury the potted plant to its rim in the fresh substrate. What could be easier?

Hot Rocks: Just Say No!

Hot rocks used to be immensely popular among herp hobbyists as heating sources for their reptiles. Made of polymer or cement, these stones are highly prone to overheating, underheating, or otherwise malfunctioning. When a hot rock goes awry, your dragon runs the risk of serious burns or even electric shock from the faulty wiring in the stone's inner heating coil. With all the other (and much more reliable) forms of artificial heating on the market today, heating rocks are absolutely unnecessary in the bearded dragon terrarium.

Hide Box

Another essential component of the bearded dragon terrarium is the hide box or shelter. In the wild, bearded dragons have a great many natural enemies: monitor lizards, birds of prey, snakes, wild hogs, and dingoes will all prey upon these lizards. Because beardies are not venomous, nor are they equipped to fight off most attackers, their primary defense is to run and hide in a rocky crevasse, hole, or other dark, snug retreat until the danger has passed. In captivity, this instinctual need for seclusion, darkness, and a sense of security must not be ignored or underestimated by hobbyists. Bearded dragons must, at all phases during their lifetime, have access to one or more hide locations within their terrarium.

As you might guess, baby and juvenile specimens need these structures the most, though adults still require hides as well. Even those very old, relaxed, dog-tame specimens need a dark, quiet place in which to escape the world and chill out every now and again.

In this cage, cinder blocks are used for hiding and climbing areas and the substrate is newspaper.

The good news is that hide boxes or retreats can be made out of just about anything: broken clay pot-halves, slabs of cork bark, wooden planks nailed together to fashion a small shelter, store-bought herp hide boxes, etc. As long as it provides enough shelter for your bearded dragon to completely remove itself from view, your lizard won't care what the hide box is made of. Of course, if you've got a taste for the naturalistic look, there are seemingly endless varieties of synthetic hide boxes available through pet shops and herp-specialty websites. Artificial logs and stumps, polymer or ceramic caverns, and plastic stone-heaps are just a few of the myriad hides available in the pet trade.

When placing hide boxes around your dragon's terrarium, remember that providing seclusion and safety to your lizard is your ultimate goal. Situate the hides such that minimal amounts of light can get in; the darker the interior of the hide is, the more your beardie will like it. Angle the entry way to the hide box away from visible traffic. That is, turn the hide doorway such that human movements in the room will not be visible to your dragon (perhaps facing a back wall of the tank), as the commotion of hobbyists and their friends may stress a dragon that is seeking true seclusion.

In large terrariums housing more than one dragon, you'll definitely need multiple hides; at least one per animal. Even in single-dragon tanks, it is highly advisable to place two or more hides in various locations around the tank, as beardies seem to relish choice in their hideaways. I've found it beneficial to place one hide directly above an undertank heating pad, and to place a second one toward the cooler end of the tank. The heated hide will provide ample seclusion to the lizard, while still offering sufficient warmth to aid in digestion and metabolism, while the non-heated hide will provide darkness, quiet, and cool for the animal. Since bearded dragons may move from warmer to cooler (and vice versa) locations many times throughout the day in the wild, this duality of hiding places closely

simulates what these dragons are instinctually accustomed to and allows for excellent thermoregulation. You dragon will not have to choose between being able to hide and being at the temperature it prefers.

In terraria housing multiple dragons, be sure you include multiple hiding and basking areas.

Heating and Lighting

The matter of heating and lighting in the bearded dragon terrarium is one that is deserving of more than a little attention. The Australian Outback is a hot, sunny, arid place, and in order for dragons to thrive in captivity, hobbyists must maintain captive conditions that closely simulate these natural conditions.

Daily ambient temperatures inside your dragon's terrarium should, therefore, remain between 80° and 84°F (26.7° to 28.9°C). At one end of the terrarium, provide a basking spot that reaches 95° to 100°F (35° to 37.8°C), and at the other, provide a dark, cool retreat, so that your dragon may thermoregulate as necessary.

Light Bulbs

Heat may be supplied to your beardie in several ways. Incandescent heating lamps (sometimes sold as dome lamps or clamp lamps) provide both light and substantial heat to your dragon. Place the lamp atop the screen lid toward one end of the terrarium. Directly beneath this lamp place a large, flat rock or a climbing branch, which will become your dragon's primary basking spot. It is important that your dragon does not have direct access to this lamp, as the bulb will get very hot and should it come into direct contact with your beardie, serious burns or even death may result.

The wattage of the bulb you use in this lamp will vary based on two factors: the lamp's distance away from the terrarium, and the size of the terrarium to be heated. If your heating lamp is suspended more than about 10 to 12 inches (25.4 to 30.5 cm) above the terrarium, then a higher wattage bulb will be necessary to convey enough heat into the tank. Similarly, if you are trying to maintain a warm ambient temperature within a 150-gallon (568 l) tank, a larger bulb or multiple heating lamps will be necessary to heat such a voluminous terrarium. The inverse is also true. A lamp that is less than 10 inches (25.4 cm) away from the terrarium's basking site can be of a lower wattage, while a smaller terrarium will not require so many bulbs to adequately heat it. To provide the necessary temperature range, you will probably have to experiment with different bulb wattages.

Because incandescent bulbs create such intense light, they are not fit for heating your dragons at night. Maintain adequately warm conditions at night by using one or more night cycle bulbs. Crafted out of dark purple or deep red glass, these low-wattage bulbs emit a smooth, gentle warmth and cast only the faintest of glows into the terrarium. These will not impose upon you dragon's sleeping habits. Deserts and other beardie habitats cool off significantly at night, and you should mimic this temperature cycle in the terrarium. Nighttime temperatures can safely drop to 65° to 70°F (18.3° to 21.1°C). In many homes, the keeper will not need to provide any supplemental heat at night beyond an undertank heating pad (see below for details on these heating devices).

Heat Emitters

A second method of heating, which is similar in nature to the heating lamp, is the ceramic heat emitter. Shaped roughly like a bell, these items are composed of a metal heating coil encased in a heavy-duty ceramic shell. They screw into incandescent fixtures. They come in varying wattages and can emit tremendous amounts of heat—much more than an equally sized light bulb—yet they cast no light. Because they produce so much heat, heat emitters must only be used in ceramic bulb fixtures. Many pet stores that carry reptiles sell these fixtures. They can also be found at hardware stores and online.

Ceramic heat emitters are excellent for maintaining warm temperatures at night, as they cast no light to disturb your dragon. Hobbyists who employ florescent lighting fixtures may wish to add heat to the tank by way of a heat emitter. If another light source is employed, ceramic heat emitters can also be used to create a basking spot in the terrarium, or, when used in lower wattages, can be used in place of night cycle bulbs to maintain warm nightly temperatures. As is true of the light bulbs, security steps must be taken to ensure that your dragon cannot come into direct contact with the heat emitter. Because they get so hot, a burn from a ceramic heat emitter can be a sudden and ghastly event.

Bearded dragons require both heat lamps and ultraviolet lights to maintain their health in the terrarium.

About Glass

Be aware that glass (window glass, the glass walls of the terrarium, etc.) filters out necessary UV wavelengths of light, so placing your dragon or its terrarium near a sunny window is not a substitute for real or artificial UV radiation. Moreover, the placing of a terrarium near a window is a bad idea, for while the UV radiation will not pass through, copious amounts of heat will. A terrarium can easily overheat and literally cook its inhabitants if it is left in a sunny window or in any area that gets direct sunlight.

Undertank Heating Pads

Another excellent source of heat is the undertank heating pad. Manufactured with a smooth side and an adhesive side, these pads adhere to the outside bottom of the terrarium, and they convey a gentle, even warmth up through the substrate of the terrarium, thereby heating your dragon from beneath. Heating pads are rendered useless, however, if the substrate above them is layered too thick. Within my own beardie environs, I find that a heating pad situated directly beneath a thin portion of substrate makes a favorite napping spot for my dragons; the lizards curl up above the pad and doze for long, warm, comfortable hours.

Mix and Match

Individually, all of these heating methods— basking lamps, ceramic heat emitters, and undertank heating pads—will generate some degree of heat, but if the hobbyist is to truly simulate the dragon's natural environs, a combination of heat sources will usually be necessary. Suspend an incandescent basking lamp by day above the basking site, use an undertank heating pad underneath this to create a nice hot spot, and employ a low-powered ceramic heat emitter after dark so as to maintain nightly temperatures of 65° to 75°F (18.3° to 23.9°C).

No matter what heating apparatus you use, be sure to employ a thermometer inside the terrarium so as to accurately track the temperature. Never try to guess what the temperature is in your beardie's terrarium, for what you think is warm enough might fall short of the dragon's requirements. The inverse of this is even more dangerous; temperatures that are too low will result in slow detriment, while temperatures that are too high can overheat and literally cook your dragon to death in a matter of minutes. Digital thermometers are the most accurate, and the ones that store the high and low temperatures provide you with information even when you are not observing the terrarium directly.

Ultraviolet Light

While one form of heating can largely substitute for another as long as certain temperatures are attained, superior lighting is not so negotiable. Over the eons, bearded dragons developed metabolic systems that do not function properly without ample exposure to ultraviolet radiation (UV), which naturally enters the Earth's atmosphere with the rays of the sun. The result is that these lizards are sun-lovers, spending hours each day basking in the sun's rays. Without this exposure to UV rays, your bearded dragon will soon develop myriad disorders, metabolic bone disease (MBD) being chief among them.

If you live in a warm area of the globe, you should set aside at least one or two hours each week to take your dragon outside and let it bask in natural sunlight. Any more time you can spend with your dragon in the sun is definitely beneficial (this is a great time to bond with your pet and observe some of its natural behaviors), but one to two hours a week is the minimum time allotment for ensuring a healthy dragon.

Other UV Bulbs

There are now incandescent bulbs that supply ultraviolet B. These tend to be expensive, but they last a long time, so it is more economical in the long term to buy these instead of a fluorescent bulb that will need to be replaced every six months or so. The problem with these bulbs is that they generate a lot of heat and do not normally come in wattages lower than 60 watts. Therefore, they cannot be used in smaller cages. These UV incandescents are otherwise excellent products. You can find them on the Internet and at pet stores that have good reptile supply sections.

When indoors, exposure to artificial UV radiation may be achieved by outfitting your dragon's enclosure with a florescent UV bulb. Full-spectrum UV bulbs are sold in most pet shops as reptile bulbs or under a similar name. Make sure the bulb you purchase offers at least 5 to 7 percent UVA and UVB radiation. UVA radiation helps your dragon to remain mentally healthy, stimulated, and to maintain a hearty appetite. UVB radiation, on the other hand, is integral in the dragon's ability to metabolize vitamin D3 and calcium. Without ample exposure to wavelengths of UVB radiation, a bearded dragon will develop a deficiency of vitamin D3 and soon thereafter will show the degenerative symptoms of MBD.

Some varieties of bulb, often sold as plant grow-lights, are not suitable, as they do not provide the full-spectrum UV lighting your dragon needs. Bearded dragons of all ages and all species need at least 10 to 12 hours of exposure to real or artificial UVA and

UVB radiation daily if they are to thrive. If denied access to UV rays for even a few weeks time, your dragon will begin showing signs of distress. Rig these fluorescent UV lights such that at least one (preferably two) bulb illuminates the length of the terrarium. This will ensure that ample UV rays reach all corners of the terrarium. To provide their benefits, they need to be no more than 12 to 18 inches (30.5 to 45.7 cm) away from your dragons.

Bear in mind that glass, even one pane such as the wall of your terrarium, will filter out nearly all of the UV radiation cast by a UV light bulb or cast by the sun. Even a fine-mesh screen lid may filter out as much as 30 to 35 percent of all UV rays. If your UV fixture is going to do your dragon any good, it must be allowed to shine directly upon the dragon, with no glass, plastic, or acrylic (and minimal screen) to shield the rays. Using a broader-mesh screen is, therefore, preferable over a finer-mesh screen. UV light bulbs also have a life expectancy of about one year. As time passes, a bulb's output of UV rays is gradually diminished, and, at the one year mark, these special bulbs are little more than regular light bulbs with a virtually non-existent output of UVA or UVB radiation. Changing the UV light bulbs every 6 to 8 months ensures maximum efficiency and UV exposure for bearded dragons, and changing the bulbs once a year should be considered the minimum.

Outdoor Housing

Many hobbyists that live in warm areas (or at least seasonally warm areas) house their bearded dragons outdoors. While the outdoor pen will allow your animals to live very much like they would in the wild, great care and planning must go into the establishment of such a pen. Outdoor pens allow the dragons to soak up as much ultraviolet radiation as they like, they allow for ventilation and air flow that cannot be matched in any indoor enclosure, and they encourage natural behaviors. Outdoor pens are also excellent places to house multiple dragons, as a large pen

Usually, the best method for heating bearded dragons is to have both overhead lights and undertank heating pads.

will afford plenty of hides, perches, and territory for a whole colony of dragons.

The first hurdle to be conquered, however, is the geographic area in which you live. Bearded dragon hobbyists residing in New York State or County Cork in Ireland are best advised against building an outdoor pen for their beardies, as the cool, wet climate in these areas will not sustain bearded dragons for any length of time—although, you could build a temporary pen for housing on nice days. If you live in the deserts of the American west, central Africa, or southern Spain, however, where the climate is very similar to the beardie's native Australian habitat, then an outdoor pen might be just the thing for you. Anywhere the daily highs of summer reach close to 100°F (37.8°C), and the nightly lows do not dip below 69° to 75°F (20.6° to 23.9°C) will allow you to keep your dragons in outdoor pens. Bear in mind, however, that virtually no location aside from the Outback or central Africa can accommodate these lizards outside year-round. A great many North American hobbyists house their animals outside for 7 or perhaps 8 months out of the year, but bring them back inside for the winter.

Sunning Pool

Kiddy pools, as long as they are escape-proof, make excellent play or basking areas for one or more dragons. By placing this pool in your yard in an area of unfiltered sunlight, you can allow your dragons to bask as they would in nature. Make sure to place multiple hides in the kiddy pool, as your dragon may need to escape the direct rays of the sun. Letting your dragon bask in the kiddy pool for a few hours each week will make a tremendous difference in its activity level, appetite, color, and overall health.

Construction

There are many options for the construction of an outdoor enclosure; due to space restrictions only the basics are covered here. In most styles of outdoor enclosures, you will begin by cementing several 4 inch x 4 inch (10 cm x 10 cm) wooden posts in the ground, the pattern of which will form a rectangle (or whatever shape you desire), and constructing a doorway large enough for you to enter. Most hobbyists build a double door, an inner and outer door, so that no dragons can escape the enclosure when they enter. You can buy a screen door or make your own, depending on your building skills.

Create walls for the enclosure by stapling a fine-mesh hardware cloth along the inside of each post, making sure to close all seams and shore up any loose corners. The holes of this

A Friendly Reminder

mesh should be small enough that only your little finger can slip through; we don't want our beloved pets to escape and disappear. Because bearded dragons are excellent climbers, you'll have to place a screen mesh roof atop the enclosure as well.

Other options for constructing the enclosure include making it out of railroad ties or cinder blocks. Neither of these options are as secure as the hardware cloth cage, but they have been employed successfully by some hobbyists.

Security

Your outdoor pen needs to be secure enough to keep your dragons in, but it must also guard against unwanted intruders, such as snakes, foxes, coyotes (which can easily and quickly dig under the screen of the enclosure to wreak havoc on your dragons), hawks, skunks, cats, and other animals, depending on your location. There are certain precautions

Basking dragons will flatten out their bodies to expose as much skin to the sun (or heat lamp) as possible.

that can help prevent any predator attacks. When you cement the posts in the ground, dig a foot-deep (30.5 cm) trench in the ground between each post, making sort of a moat around the periphery of the enclosure. When you begin attaching the screen mesh to the posts, run the screen to the bottom of the trench, and then fill the trench back in with soil. Now you have a wire mesh screen running underground, which will help to stop most burrowing predators from digging under the screen to get at your dragons. Incidentally, this will also help prevent your dragons from digging out.

A second method, which I have heard works very well, is to place a double layer of screen over the lower half of each wall of the enclosure. Staple one layer on the inside of the posts, then staple another layer on the outside of those posts. Bear in mind that your dragons

Fences

If you house your dragon outdoors, you may want to fence in your yard. Having your enclosure in a fenced-in yard has several advantages. If your beardie manages to escape from the enclosure, it will now have to get through the fence as well. This may give you the time you need to find your pet. Fencing helps keep out wildlife that could harm your beardie. Additionally, it helps discourage anyone from coming into your yard and stealing or harming your dragon.

The Benefits of Trees

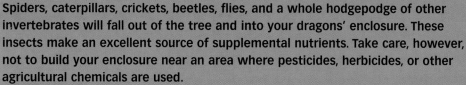

When constructing an outdoor enclosure, it is smart to build it close to a fairly large tree. Not only will this tree provide shade throughout the day, but with trees come insects. Spiders, caterpillars, crickets, beetles, flies, and a whole hodgepodge of other invertebrates will fall out of the tree and into your dragons' enclosure. These insects make an excellent source of supplemental nutrients. Take care, however, not to build your enclosure near an area where pesticides, herbicides, or other agricultural chemicals are used.

I've even seen some enclosures in which flowering plants are added, thereby attracting a host of insects into the enclosure within reach of the hungry dragons. The dragons will also eat the flowers themselves.

Mixing and Matching

Take care in how you mix dragons in an outdoor enclosure, as territorial bouts between rival males can still be problematic, even when it seems each animal has ample space and territory. As is true within the indoor terrarium enclosure, the mixing of specimens of radically varying sizes is simply not a good idea, as juveniles housed with old adults are likely to be sorely bullied. House juveniles with juveniles and adults with adults.

will be totally confined by the inner layer of screen and will not be able to come into contact with this outer layer of screen. Attach to this outer layer (a band of screen running perhaps half-way up each wall) an electrified fence unit.

The result is that any predator that comes near the enclosure will, upon touching the outer screen, get a fierce charge of electricity, and will think twice before trying to snack on your beardies again! Take care, however, that there is no physical contact between the inner and outer layers of screen, as the same electric current that is supposed to protect your dragons could do them great harm if your enclosure is incorrectly wired. Some hobbyists use rubber insulators to keep the electricity flowing through only the outer screen and never through the inner one.

The Interior

Once you've constructed and secured your outdoor enclosure, it's time to outfit it. Large rocks, cinder blocks, wooden logs and other climbing material, and ample hides are virtually all that your dragons will require. More or fewer of these items will be needed based on how many dragons you house in the

The primary benefit of housing your beardie outdoors is the exposure to natural sunlight.

enclosure. Ideally, your enclosure will get a large amount of direct sunlight each day, and there will be plenty of room for all your dragons to bask. If, however, the enclosure only gets a limited amount of sunlight, you'll want to make sure that each dragon gets access to some direct rays. Building multiple-tiered perches out of logs or boards is a good way to create

Because outdoor enclosures are usually larger than indoor ones, they allow you to house more dragons in them.

perching/basking sites for numerous dragons. Although they do love the sun, be sure to include shady areas, so that the dragons can regulate their own temperatures. The beardies are likely to dig their own cool retreats, too.

Including some live plants in the outdoor enclosure enhances the appearance and provides your dragons with some food. Be aware that plants may need to be replaced periodically as your beardies consume and trample them. Any of the plants listed as food in the feeding section can be planted in the outdoor enclosure, depending on your climate. Plants that can withstand dry conditions are the best choices because you don't want the enclosure to become too humid.

Large, shallow water dishes are also a necessity, as your dragons will need to drink more often when housed out-of-doors. Placing numerous water dishes at various locations about the enclosure is preferable to placing only one centrally located dish, as once the one dish becomes soiled, the dragons' only source of water is contaminated until you change it.

The same holds true of feeding dishes. Placing two or three about the enclosure is better than using a single, larger dish, as any dominant animals will bully their smaller, weaker counterparts away from the food. By incorporating multiple food and water dishes, you ensure that all residents get equal access to the life-sustaining nutrients.

How Many?

While many species of reptiles and amphibians can successfully be housed in pairs or colonies within the same enclosure, bearded dragons should, ideally, be housed individually.

When housing your dragon outdoors, remember to provide shade as well as basking areas.

By their very nature, bearded dragons are territorial animals, and hierarchies are established in the wild that allow the largest males to establish the largest territories. During the mating season, females may pass freely through a male's range, but rival, trespassing males will be met with head-bobbing, beard-billowing, and other threats of violence if they come too close.

In captivity, these behaviors are also exhibited. If an especially large terrarium or enclosure is being used, then multiple dragons may be kept together, though each lizard must be supplied with its own climbing branches, heating apparatus, and hides, as the natural hierarchy will allow only the dominant dragon to have access to the best climbs, hides, etc. To avoid domination of an alpha male at the dinner table, multiple food dishes placed at various locations throughout the terrarium will ensure that each individual animal gets plenty to eat. It is generally accepted that a 125-gallon (473 l) terrarium, outfitted properly, will provide ample room for only two adult dragons or three juveniles. Overcrowding in the bearded dragon enclosure will lead to a cascade of negative side effects, including increased stress levels in the dragons, depressed immune systems, loss of appetites, and aggression among tankmates. It is not unheard of for the largest dragon within a multiple-dragon enclosure to violently lash out, nipping, biting, and possibly mauling its weaker counterparts.

Dragons of varying sizes (i.e., adults and juveniles) should never be housed in the same enclosure, no matter how large the cage is, as a bout of territorial violence can easily result in the injury, mutilation, or even (albeit rarely) the death of the smaller dragon. Adult dragons may also see newborns or small juveniles as food items, and they may eat their intended cagemates. Even similarly sized dragons, if housed in tight enclosures, may engage in brutal, territorial combat.

It has been my experience that housing multiple females in a single enclosure typically results in a more peaceful, less confrontational coexistence between the captives, while male cohabitants tend to display much more frequent aggressive behaviors. These aggressive behaviors, at least within my own experiences, are particularly prevalent among 3 to 6 year-old males. I believe this stems from the burgeoning social dominance that animals within this age range must exhibit in the wild if they are to spread their genes.

Even in a large outdoor enclosure, males may be aggressive to each other. House only one male per cage.

Chapter 4

Feeding

Feeding time is easily one of the highlights of any bearded dragon experience. Young and beginning hobbyists in particular relish their bearded dragon's delightful, almost comical display of enthusiasm at the dinner table. Young dragons will circle their prey and visibly prepare by wiggling their little bodies, craning their necks, and gauging distance before making the final, lunging attack. Adults put on no less of a show by charging in, mouth agape, and utterly mauling any live foods in sight! Because feeding a beardie is never boring, this time can be a great opportunity to fully appreciate your dragon. Hand feeding crickets is a fun way to interact with your pet. Be warned, however, that hungry adult and sub-adult beardies are so enthusiastic that they may not be able to distinguish between a tender cricket and a keeper's fingertip! Feeding tongs or leather gloves are often necessary to safeguard against being bitten.

Natural Diet

In the wild, bearded dragons are opportunistic omnivores whose diet depends largely on what food source is available at the time. When in a densely vegetated area, a wild beardie will consume leaves, shoots, tender stems, berries, fruits, seeds, and a host of other plant matter. Should that same individual find itself in an area rich in insect life, it would happily gorge itself on whatever invertebrates were unfortunate enough to cross the dragon's path. Large adult dragons will also take mice, small birds, other lizards, and even small snakes should the opportunity present itself. Such a wide variety of prey and greens helps ensure that the dragon receives all the necessary vitamins, minerals, and nutrients it needs to flourish and remain healthy.

Pet Diet

While it is impossible to perfectly simulate this wide variety of fare in the captive environment, we can come close by offering as many live animal and vegetable materials as possible. Prey items can include crickets, mealworms, wax worms, fruit flies, superworms, roaches, pinkie mice, small lizards (anoles and house geckos), and adult mice. Vegetable matter may include green and red cabbage, kale, collard greens, carrots and carrot tops, mustard greens, arugula, parsley, okra, bell peppers, alfalfa sprouts, peeled grapes, green beans, mixed frozen vegetables, romaine lettuce, green peas, and hibiscus and dandelion leaves and flowers, which must be pesticide and fertilizer free. Feed mostly the leafy items and include other items for variety. A quick and easy way to prepare all of these vegetables is to simply use a food processor and coarsely chop them. A handheld cheese grater also works well in amply dicing up vegetable matter, particularly hard items such as carrots, sweet potatoes, and squashes.

Processed and canned herp foods can also be offered, but sparingly as these products may not provide the variety of foods dragons need, nor do they offer a sustainable balance of nutrients. I offer my dragons canned or processed foods no more than once every week,

Bearded dragons are opportunistic omnivores that will eat a wide range of plants and animals.

as a diet too rich in commercial processed foods can quickly lead to obesity.

Gut-Loading

It's important to remember that most feeder items do not supply all the nutrients that bearded dragons need. In order to offset nutritional imbalances, hobbyists are advised to gut-load all prey items before offering them to their beardies. Gut-loading is a 48-hour process in which feeder items, primarily crickets and mealworms, are placed in a separate container, the floor of which is covered with tropical fish food, dried puppy kibble, and/or instant baby cereal. For water and added nutrition, include some vegetables such as carrots, sweet potatoes, orange slices, and the stems of leafy greens.

During the next 48 hours, the insects will consume these highly nutritious foods, and, when they are fed to your beardie, will transfer those added nutrients to your pet. Feeding gut-loaded insects to young and ailing dragons can make a significant difference in the growth or recovery rate of the lizards. Herp-specific vitamin and mineral supplements can also be sprinkled into the gut-load food mixture. I highly recommend the practice of gut-loading to any and all bearded dragon hobbyists.

Vitamins and Minerals

As well as other nutrients, vitamins and minerals also play vital roles in the growth and long-term health of your bearded dragon. Most notable among these are vitamin D3 and calcium, which are integral to the proper formation of strong bones and teeth, and which are also critical to the development of egg shells in gravid females. Bear in mind that both calcium and D3 must be given simultaneously as beardies cannot adequately metabolize calcium if their intake of vitamin D3 is too low.

The amount of calcium and D3 you give your dragon hinges on how much natural sunlight the animal receives and the age of the animal. Remember that the ultraviolet

A Note About Wax Worms

Wax worms are parasites of beehives that consume beeswax and honey. Because of their specialized diet, it is difficult to gut-load them. They are best fed to the dragons within a few days of purchase. Also, these insects are high in fat and are best fed sparingly, unless you are trying to put weight on a beardie quickly.

radiation in sunlight stimulates production of vitamin D3 in the beardie's skin. Adult specimens housed in outdoor enclosures that receive lots of unfiltered sunlight will need less supplementation, perhaps only once each week. Hatchling specimens (to 4 months old) require daily supplements of D3 and calcium, and juvenile specimens (4 to 18 months old) need 3 to 4 supplemented meals per week.

Take care in which type of calcium supplement you offer, as those powders containing phosphorous should have at least a 2:1 calcium to phosphorous ratio, 3:1 is even better. Also

Leafy greens are among the most nutritious foods you can feed to your beardie.

be careful in offering other vitamins and minerals to your dragon. Given in excess, some vitamins can become harmful to your lizard. Vitamin A, for example, is retained in the dragon's body and can become toxic if given too frequently; to avoid vitamin A toxicity, use a supplement that contains beta carotene instead of other forms of the vitamin. Use a multivitamin supplement no more than twice each week for hatchlings, and once each week for juvenile and adult specimens. Be sure to use a vitamin and mineral supplement that is manufactured specifically for use with reptiles. Do not use supplements designed for birds, dogs, or other animals.

Feeding Schedule

By closely monitoring how much your dragon eats and when, you can keep a handle on how fast it should grow and what nutrients might be lacking, while at the same time thwarting overfeeding and obesity. Of course, not all beardies are the same, and at various stages of their life their food and nutrition requirements are different. For this reason, I have delineated three different sample feeding schedules, one each respectively for the hatchling, juvenile, and adult specimens. Feed as many insects as your bearded dragon will consume in five minutes.

Hatchlings

The hatchling period is easily the stage of the beardie's life during which the animal is most fragile. It is critical that during this time the lizard receives ample nutrients. The term hatchling here refers to those animals that are less than 4 to 5 months old. The amount of food that a hatchling receives is important, but the size of the food is also critical. Hatchlings must *never be offered prey items larger than their heads.* Feeding larger prey can cause a hatchling serious injury, disability, or death. Fruit flies, pinhead and one-quarter grown crickets, and the smallest wax worms are all good choices.

Because of their voracious appetites, hatchling dragons will try to consume prey that is too large. A baby beardie that consumes a food item that is too big may slip into a state of paralysis or it may even die. Mealworms seem to

Beardies will use their sticky tongues to catch small insects, although their tongues are not as specialized for the task as a chameleon's.

be especially problematic, and feeding them to hatchling beardies quite often results in paralysis. *Never offer mealworms* to bearded dragons that are less than 4 or 5 months old.

Because they are in a stage of rapid growth, hatchling dragons have different nutritional needs than do adults, just like human babies. They should receive a higher percentage of insects and other animal protein in their diets than adults. The diet of a young dragon should comprise 60 to 80 percent animal protein and 20 to 40 percent vegetable matter, while an adult, on the other hand, needs a diet of only 20 to 25 percent animal protein and 75 to 80 percent vegetables.

Because of their rapid metabolism during this stage of life, hatchling beardies must be fed several times each day. Offer tiny insects three to four times each day. Dust one meal per day in calcium/D3 supplement if you have not already added these supplements to the gut-loading mixture. If you feed exclusively gut-loaded feeders that have received vitamin/mineral supplements, no additional dusting is necessary.

You should offer finely chopped vegetable matter at least three times weekly; daily is best. Make sure that these vegetable materials are finely grated or shredded.

Bear in mind that some days your beardie will be hungrier than others. Some heavy feedings on Monday might result in the beardie accepting less food on Tuesday. This is okay. Young beardies are in a rapid stage of growth, and they will eat according to their metabolic needs. A properly housed, amply heated, healthy baby beardie, however, is rarely shy at the dinner plate. Remember also that because the metabolism of your baby beardie is so high and its reserves are low, it is critical that you not miss a feeding. Unlike juvenile and adult specimens, a baby bearded dragon can literally starve to

It is very important to offer hatchlings only tiny prey. In this picture, the cricket looks like it may be too large for the baby dragon.

death in a matter of a few days. Offer your dragon all its regularly scheduled meals, even if it refuses to eat or does not appear hungry.

If you are housing multiple beardie babies in a single enclosure, it is important that each individual gets enough to eat. It is common for the larger, stronger hatchlings to bully their weaker brothers and sisters away from the table at mealtime. If they do not get enough to eat, the smaller dragons will quickly wither and perish. Prevent this scenario by separating your dragons at feeding time, if necessary.

Juveniles

Once your dragon is 4 to 5 months old, it is considered to be in the juvenile stage of life and you can decrease the frequency of feedings. Juvenile refers to those animals that are 5 to 18 months old.

Juvenile beardies have grown in mass and have some fat reserves, so feeding them three times a day is no longer necessary. Moreover, since their rate of growth is also slowing down, juvenile beardies must not be fed so frequently, as this will make the animals obese and unhealthy. One insect feeding per day coupled with at least four vegetable feedings per week is all a juvenile beardie requires. A wide variety of fare coupled with regular vitamin and mineral supplementation, however, is still necessary. Supplement one meal per week with broad spectrum vitamin supplement, and three meals per week with calcium/D3 powder.

Because they are larger and stronger than they were as hatchlings, juvenile beardies may all be offered some of the foods that were off limits to the hatchlings. Their diet can now include mealworms and pinkie mice (offered only once every 2 to 3 weeks). Remember that all prey items should be smaller than the dragon's head. It is also important that you begin increasing the amount of vegetable matter that your dragon consumes and slightly decreasing the amount of animal proteins that it ingests.

Adults

Once your beardie reaches the adult stage, which is 18 months old or older, it has the most lax feeding schedule of its entire life. With the exception of breeding females, adult

Picky Dragons

Sometimes a picky beardie will eat only select vegetables from its dish, avoiding other vegetables that might not suit his taste. In the long term, this may cause a nutritional imbalance. Thwart this by thoroughly chopping and mixing the vegetables in the dish, thus making it more difficult for your dragon to pick out his favorites.

Sample Feeding Record

A sample of what a week's feeding for a baby beardie might be:

Monday	9:00 am	Fed 3 pinhead crickets dusted in vitamin/calcium/D3
	Noon	Fed 2 pinhead crickets
	4:00 pm	Fed 2 pinhead crickets
Tuesday	9:00 am	Fed 5 fruit flies dusted in calcium/D3
	Noon	Fed chopped kale/mixed vegetables
	4:00 pm	Fed 3 pinhead crickets, chopped grapes/kale
Wednesday	9:00 am	Fed 3 pinhead crickets dusted in calcium/D3
	Noon	Fed 2 pinhead crickets
	4:00 pm	Fed 1 wax worm
Thursday	9:00 am	Fed 6 fruit flies dusted in calcium/D3
	Noon	Fed chopped kale/alfalfa
	4:00 pm	Fed 1 wax worm
Friday	9:00 am	Fed 2 pinhead crickets dusted in vitamin/calcium/D
	Noon	Fed 3 pinhead crickets
	4:00 pm	Fed 3 pinhead crickets
Saturday	9:00 am	Fed 3 pinhead crickets dusted in calcium/D3
	Noon	Fed chopped alfalfa/grapes/romaine lettuce
	4:00 pm	Fed 2 pinhead crickets
Sunday	9:00 am	Fed 4 pinhead crickets dusted in calcium/D3
	Noon	Fed 1 pinhead cricket
	4:00 pm	Fed 6 fruit flies

bearded dragons may be sustained on a rotating diet of insects and vegetables offered daily to every other day, with vitamin/calcium/D3 supplements added once each week.

Adult specimens can also be offered pinkies, adult mice, canned dog food, and small lizards as *occasional treats*; no more than one treat every 3 weeks to a month. Adult beardies are especially prone to obesity, so watch your dragon's rate and adjust the amount of food if necessary.

Feed your dragon the widest possible variety of foods. This dragon is being given peas, carrots, and soaked rabbit pellets.

Catching Food

A great many hobbyists feed their beardies wild-caught insects, such as grasshoppers, locusts, spiders, beetles, and moths. While this is a viable and money-saving option, you must be careful of several things. You must be absolutely sure that your source for insects is pesticide-free. Herbicides, pesticides, fertilizers, and other agricultural chemicals that have been sprayed on crops and fields may adhere to the insects you capture and can easily poison and kill your beardie when it consumes the tainted insects. Additionally, you should become familiar with any toxic insects that live in your area. Such insects as fireflies, lubber grasshoppers, and many caterpillars are toxic, and eating these bugs will make your beardie sick or worse.

Issues of Feeding

When feeding live prey to your bearded dragon, the problem of escape immediately presents itself. Crickets allowed to range freely throughout the beardie's terrarium will quickly scurry behind stones, under logs, or to some other place where they will escape your dragon. Feeding crickets one at the time is a viable option; with only one moving target on which to focus, your dragon should have no trouble zeroing in for the kill. Injured, sickly, or very young dragons can be fed single crickets with feeding tongs to avoid the stress and activity of hunting live prey.

Another reason that you should never allow crickets to roam freely in the terrarium is that if your dragon isn't hungry it will not eat, and any uneaten crickets in the terrarium will nibble or chew on the dragon. While this may sound far-fetched, bear in mind that crickets are voracious omnivores, and a horde of hungry crickets can do serious damage to a hapless dragon that, being confined to its terrarium, has no way to escape from the tiny

Bad Bugs

Although most insects, worms, arachnids, and other invertebrates you may find in your yard or garden make good food for bearded dragons, you should avoid some species. These species are toxic, vicious, or otherwise dangerous to feed to your pet.

- Ants
- Bees, wasps, hornets
- Caterpillars (depending on species)
- Centipedes
- Fireflies
- Lubber grasshoppers
- Scorpions

attackers. Even if the crickets do not chew on your dragon, a mass of these six-legged invaders climbing all over your dragon will stress your pet.

Mealworms also present escape problems in the terrarium. When placed directly on the substrate, mealworms will quickly burrow beneath the substrate and will remain there, permanently safe from your dragon. Prevent this by placing all varieties of worm in a steep-sided dish from which they cannot escape. With all the worm isolated in one dish, your dragon will be able to feed at its own leisure. Wax worms and pinkie mice may also be presented in this manner.

What About Bob?

One of the first bearded dragons I ever owned was named Bob. When he was about 18 months old, I started feeding him grasshoppers that I captured from a nearby field. Bob absolutely loved these new insects, and he always ate each and every grasshopper I offered. At the onset of fall, I harvested as many as I could, and I put them in the freezer, but this supply of wild-caught insects hardly lasted a month. When they were all gone, and I had to return to feeding pet shop feeders, Bob refused to eat. He snubbed crickets, and he turned up his nose at mealworms and vegetables. After dining on such exquisite fare as wild grasshoppers, Bob never again ate crickets, mealworms, wax worms, or any other feeder, and he took far too little vegetable matter to sustain him. After months of my force-feeding Bob with a syringe and using appetite stimulants, Bob finally expired of starvation.

So take care, my readers, that you never offer your pet a feeder-type that you cannot supply year-round. Also, keep offering the pet store and produce department staples along with the stuff you catch. Beardies can be fickle animals, and you never know when yours might develop a taste for a certain food. You certainly don't want your pet to suffer the same fate as my dear Bob.

Water

Being desert-dwelling animals, bearded dragons are well adapted to obtaining most of their water from the insects and succulent plants they consume. In captivity, however, it is necessary that you supply your dragon with a shallow dish of clean, fresh water. Rinse this dish daily, as standing water is a perfect medium for bacterial and fungal growth, and allowing your dragon to drink from a filthy dish is inviting illness. Take care that your dish is not so deep that your dragon could fall in and not escape; this is especially important in the case of hatchling dragons. Because dragons cannot tolerate high levels of humidity, you must also make sure that the water, as it evaporates from the dish, does not significantly increase the relative humidity inside the terrarium. Employ as small a water dish as is practical in a well-ventilated terrarium to avoid problems.

Chapter 5

Handling and Grooming

Aside from this lizard's prehistoric appearance, it is the handling of the bearded dragon that makes this species so appealing. Beardies seem to love handling and petting almost as much as dogs do. A beardie may spend hours sitting quietly atop its keeper's shoulder or open palm, just soaking up that mammalian body heat and being stroked over its scaly back. This handle-friendly disposition makes the beardie a particularly desired species among children and anyone who wishes to have a physical connection to his or her pet dragon. But, as is true of any animal or pet, there are certain rules of handling that must be followed to ensure the continued health and happiness of both the bearded dragon and its keeper.

Hatchlings and Young Dragons

Baby beardies are by far the most delicate dragons. At this critical juncture of life, the baby dragons are very fragile and must be handled delicately, if they are handled at all. It is best if the hobbyist refrains from needlessly handling a young dragon until it is at least four to five weeks old.

If handling a newborn or very young specimen is absolutely necessary, it is important that you never grab or suddenly grasp at the lizard, for its bones are fragile and can easily break. A tight squeeze can also cause internal damage to the lizard's organs. The solution here is to slowly (so as not to startle the young dragon) lower your hand into the terrarium and let it rest, palm up, on the substrate. Using the other hand, gently corral the baby dragon into your open palm, letting it walk freely into your waiting hand. Gently close your fingers around the dragon and raise your hand out of the terrarium.

Never hold young dragons—or any age dragon, for that matter—high off the ground, as a sudden movement could startle your lizard, causing it to jump and fall a great distance. Handle young dragons directly over a table or a soft bed, so that if your lizard does escape your grasp, it doesn't fall far or hit hard. When you return the young dragon to its terrarium, again corral the lizard into your open palm, close your hand around it, lower your hand into the terrarium, open your hand, and allow the dragon to freely crawl back into its habitat of its own accord.

Do's and Don'ts

Once your dragon is older than three to four months, it will be considerably more robust and can withstand the rigors of normal handling. It should be noted, however, that the dragon should leave and re-enter its terrarium on its terms and not on the keeper's. For example, a dragon that is clinging to a climbing branch should not be pulled and tugged on until it lets go. The handler should simply try to coax the animal off its perch or wait until the dragon is sitting on the sand before attempting to take the animal out and handle it. Quickly plucking a

It is often better to encourage hatchlings to crawl onto your hand, rather than picking the tiny lizards up.

dragon from its perch can result in injury to the animal's claws and legs.

Similarly, anyone who is not familiar with the anatomy of lizards should be aware that the tail of the bearded dragon can easily break off. While the tail will grow back in a darker, oddly scaled form, it's best that the hobbyist never attempt to grasp the animal by the tail or put undue pressure on it, as a broken tail is a bloody and painful experience that you should not put your dragon through if it can be avoided.

Many hobbyists use handling time to take their dragons outside to soak up some sunlight. Others hand-feed their dragons during this time. It should be noted, however, that while feeding small amounts of food to your dragon during handling is okay, full meals should only be offered while the animal is in its enclosure, as handling a dragon on a full stomach can cause digestive problems or even regurgitation. Do not handle your dragon for at least three to four hours after feeding it.

Proper handling periods should last for as long as both you and your dragon are comfortable with the interaction. Under normal circumstances, a bearded dragon will relish the gentle warmth coming from your body as it rests quietly atop your lap or hands. Comfortable beardies should appear alert and conscious of your every move, though not frightened or skittish. It is

Pet Your Pet

Remember to handle your dragon frequently. Frequent handling will maintain the friendliness of your dragon and may lower his stress level by providing novel experiences and interaction. If we want our dragons to truly be pets, we have to take them out and pet them.

When holding your dragon, support as much of its weight as possible; don't let it dangle.

also normal for a beardie to wander around, lick your hands and arms, and generally explore its surroundings while you handle it. Excessive attempts at escape, fervent clawing or scratching while being held, and other such skittish behaviors, however, are key indicators that the dragon is not happy and should be placed back in its enclosure.

A dragon that is held for a prolonged time in a cold house may become sluggish and slow to move. This is a sign that the animal needs to be placed back into the heat of its habitat in order to maintain adequate body temperature.

Taming

Another aspect to consider is the so-called "taming" of a bearded dragon. Those individuals that may have never been handled by their previous owners or those that were incubated at excessively high temperatures may have surprisingly foul dispositions and may even attempt to bite. Couple this nippy attitude with the powerful jaws of an adult dragon, and you could walk away from a handling session with a bloody bite-wound.

Note the flared beard and opened mouth. This dragon is unhappy and should be handled cautiously, if at all.

The keys to taming such belligerent animals are determination and quick reflexes. Grasp the adult beardie around its midsection and remove it from the tank. Pet its body and stroke its back, remembering to keep your fingers well away from its mouth and teeth. After a few weeks of such unabashed handling, your dragon will soon learn that you pose no threat, and it will come to accept you as its keeper. Nearly all beardies will calm down within a month, if the keeper handles it daily. The good news is that ill-tempered bearded dragons are much like full lunar eclipses or solar flares: you know they exist, but you might well go your entire life without ever seeing one.

Hygiene

As is the case with any pet, the matter of hygiene must not be overlooked. As much as we may love our dragons and perhaps consider them members of the family, the reality of the situation is that they are animals who live in less than sterile conditions (even immaculately maintained terrariums still harbor bacteria). The skin around the dragon's claws and the gaps between the scales can harbor bacteria that can cause human illness, so it is imperative that we wash our hands with an antibacterial soap immediately after handling our dragons. Do not put any part of the dragon in your mouth, do not let it crawl on your face, do not rub your eyes or eat while handling your dragon or cleaning its cage.

While some individuals have portrayed reptiles as rampant carriers of *Salmonella*, the truth of the matter is that the handling of reptiles is no different from any other activity in which we engage everyday. We all wear shoes, but our shoes don't make us sick because we all know not to lick the soles of our shoes, for they are dirty and contain any number of bacteria and germs that could cause illness. Similarly, a great many people eat scrambled eggs in this country, but who breaks the eggs, scrambles them in the bowl, then leaves them sitting on the counter for two days before cooking and eating them? Obviously, no one is that foolish (at least, I'd like to think that no one is that foolish), and the handling of reptiles is the same way; if you can follow the rules of hygiene in the kitchen, you can follow the rules of hygiene in the reptile terrarium.

Common Sense Cautions

It is important to supervise any child who might handle a bearded dragon. Children may get rambunctious and can squeeze and injure the dragon. Also, small children like to put things into their mouths. Because of hygiene and bacteria concerns, no children should be allowed to put any part of the dragon in their mouth nor should they be allowed to put their hands in their mouth after handling without washing them first. In fact, no reptile—no matter how docile—should be allowed near a child's face.

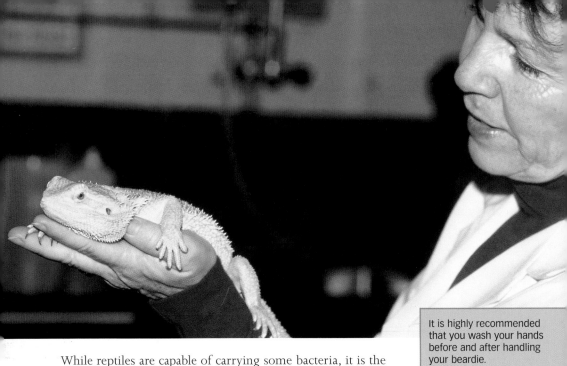

It is highly recommended that you wash your hands before and after handling your beardie.

While reptiles are capable of carrying some bacteria, it is the duty of the hobbyist to maintain a scrupulously clean environment for his or her dragon. Beardies housed under filthy conditions (feces, urine, unclean substrate, dead insects strewn about, etc.) will be much more likely to be carriers of bacteria. So washing your hands after handling your pet and maintaining clean environs will both go a long way in curbing any illness or ailment that might arise in the handling of a bearded dragon.

A responsible hobbyist will also closely observe any children when handling a dragon. By standing by and keeping a watchful eye on any junior hobbyists who are handling a dragon, the mature hobbyist can thwart both the rough mishandling of the lizard and the unsanitary practices in which a child might engage (like rubbing eyes or putting hands in the mouth while handling a dragon). Once the handling session is over, make sure that any children who have touched the dragon wash their hands thoroughly, scrubbing any areas that came into contact with the dragon. Hygiene and common sense are the keys to preventing any problems or infections when handling bearded dragons.

Hygiene is a two-way street. There are literally thousands of products that we as humans can come into contact with everyday that may prove hazardous to our beloved dragons. Perfumes, colognes, cleansers, makeup, nail polish, grease, oils, resins, and myriad other chemicals can accumulate on our hands during the day, and when we handle our dragons, they are subjected to whatever chemicals are on us. This matter is particularly important in that bearded dragons love to lick and taste their keeper's hands and skin. Not only do they externally contact what is on us, but many will ingest these chemicals as well. Therefore, it is important that the hobbyist thoroughly wash his or her hands (up to the elbow) before reaching into their pet's terrarium. Just as we do not want to get sick from any bacteria on our beardies, we certainly do not want our beardies to suffer from any chemicals or impurities that may be on our skin.

Nail-Trimming Tip

It is a good idea to keep a small container of styptic powder on hand, in case you accidentally cut your beardie's nail too short. This powerful blood-stopper can be found in drug stores and most supermarkets. In a pinch, corn starch will also work very well. Put a small amount in a jar lid or on a plate and press the bloody nail into it. Repeat as needed. The bleeding should stop shortly.

Grooming

It may be surprising that any type of grooming could ever apply to a lizard, but it can. Grooming in lizards almost entirely refers to trimming the claws. Large adult dragons can, without realizing it, inflict scratches and scrapes on their keepers. Not only can this be painful to the keeper, but a scratch that breaks the skin is subject to possible infection.

Using avian claw-clippers, trim the tip-ends of your dragon's claws off. Care must be taken when performing this, however, for a sizable vein runs into the claw. Visible as a small, pale ridge extending about half-way down the underside of each claw, this vein carries a surprising amount of blood and nerve endings, so great care must be taken not to sever it. If you do cut your dragon's claws into the quick, expect the dragon to pull away, obviously reacting to the painful wound. Hold a paper towel to the claw until the bleeding stops, and treat it with a daub of topical antiseptic cream (the pain relieving variety is best). Avoid severing the vein by only trimming the tip-end of the claw.

Chapter 6

Health Care

Bearded dragons—or any reptiles for that matter—are not disposable animals. Understanding that these animals may one day have need of specialized veterinarian care is an important prerequisite to owning a bearded dragon. It is the responsibility of the hobbyist to offer his or her pets the utmost in health care. A trip to the veterinarian when necessary definitely is a part of that health care.

Finding a Herp Vet

It is not always easy to find vets who are experienced with reptiles and amphibians. Here are some suggestions to help you locate a vet who can help with your pet bearded dragon. It is best if you locate one before you actually have an emergency.

- **Call veterinarians listed as "exotic" or "reptile" vets in the phonebook. Ask them questions to be sure they are familiar with bearded dragons.**
- **Ask at your local pet stores, zoos, and animal shelters to see if there is someone they can recommend.**
- **Herpetological societies are likely to know which local vets treat reptiles and amphibians.**
- **Contact the Association of Reptilian and Amphibian Veterinarians. Their website is www.arav.org.**

If you're a first-time dragon keeper, or if you're new to herp keeping on the whole, the first thing you'll need to do is find a good veterinarian. While vets specializing in the care of cats, dogs, and horses are common in most towns and cities, those vets specializing in scaled animals may be a little harder to find. A quick glance in the phone book, or a few minutes on the Internet, and you should be able to locate a man or woman of veterinary medicine who is skilled in treating reptiles and amphibians. Be prepared to travel a town or two away from your own.

Injuries

Injuries are among the most frequently encountered problems in bearded dragons. Take care to always keep your dragon safe from wounds, burns, and other injuries.

Burns

The first of the injuries often seen in bearded dragons are burns. Most often occurring as the result of a faulty heating stone, burns may also result from the dragon coming into direct contact with a heat lamp or ceramic heat emitter.

Burns will vary in severity, ranging from mild discoloration and blistering of the skin and scales, to open, charred, bleeding wounds. The best cure for any type of burn is prevention. Maintain an enclosure for your dragon that does not allow the animal to gain direct access to a heat lamp or ceramic heat emitter, as these fixtures can get extremely hot and can inflict disfiguring or even lethal burns in a matter of seconds. Heat stones, or hot rocks as they are also known, have a bad track record when it comes to burns. If the polymer or artificial matrix comprising the stone is thin in an area, the gentle heat of the heating coil inside can reach dangerous temperatures in that area. These flaws in the heat

Establish a relationship with a herp veterinarian before you have an emergency.

stone are notorious for burning bellies, thus heat stones should be avoided altogether.

In the event of even mild burns, a trip to the vet is in order. Burns must be treated for surface skin and scale damage, internal muscular damage, and especially for secondary infection. Serious burns will also cause severe dehydration. Antibiotic injections and topical salves comprise the standard regimen for successful recovery from burn wounds. Again, prevention is a hobbyist's best defense against burns.

Wounds

Like burns, open wounds are prime for secondary infection, and they must be disinfected to prevent this. Minor cuts, nicks, and scrapes can be treated with daily daubs of topical antiseptic cream. A triple antibiotic ointment that contains a pain reliever works well, for it not only prevents infection, but it also alleviates the dragon's pain. Any wound that is deep or debilitating or that bleeds profusely must be treated by a vet as soon as possible.

Also, like burns, wounds are better prevented than treated. Excessively abrasive décor within the dragon's enclosure may prove problematic. Lava rocks and other severely coarse items have no place in the bearded dragon habitat, as a dragon's soft underbelly is easily rubbed raw by such abrasive

Checkup

When you purchase your dragon, be sure to bring it to your veterinarian for an initial checkup. This is the first step in ensuring a long, happy, and healthy life for your new pet dragon.

substances. Rocks or pieces of wood with sharp points or edges must not be included in the cage furnishings.

Dragons that are kept in close quarters often attack and injure each other; males usually demonstrate more aggression, and females or smaller males typically are the victims. Because of the dragon's powerful jaws and sharp, serrate teeth, bite wounds are seldom mild. Usually, the victim is a snarled, bloody mess. I recommend taking any bitten or mauled animals directly to your veterinarian for immediate treatment. Avoid the temptation to treat small or mild bite wounds on your own, as the mouth of a beardie is teeming with bacteria, and infection can easily set into a beardie bite.

Dragons—especially males—can be aggressive to each other. This female lost her foot to an aggressive male and needed veterinary attention.

Snout Rubbing

As much of a behavioral issue as it is an injury, snout rubbing often results from large dragons being housed in inadequately small enclosures. As it searches for a way to escape the confines of its enclosure, a beardie may rub its snout bloody and raw. Remedy this by removing the dragon to a sterile quarantine tank and treating the raw snout with daily swabs of iodine or hydrogen peroxide to disinfect the wound.

Of course, the healing process will all be for naught if the cause of the nose rubbing is not cured as well. Normally, bearded dragons will rub themselves raw if their habitat does not meet their basic needs. Make sure to maintain proper housing conditions, diet, and adequately sized caging to discourage nose rubbing.

The occasional dragon will rub simply because it wants to explore the room around it, and it doesn't understand that no amount of searching or pushing will ever get it past the glass. Remedy this by either taking the dragon out and giving it some exercise on a daily basis or by covering three sides of the dragon's enclosure. Spray painting the outside walls of a glass aquarium black or otherwise covering them with a dark, opaque substance like contact paper or construction paper, will limit the dragon's ability to see out, thereby curbing the lizard's desire to escape or explore out into the room.

Custom-built enclosures sometimes are crafted with screen-covered ventilation holes low in their sides. If these holes are covered in metallic screen, that screen may be a source of chronic nose rubbing. Replace any metallic screens with nylon or rubberized screens, both of which are much easier on the dragon's snout should it continue to rub.

Parasites
Internal Parasites

One of the most common and daunting problems that herp hobbyists confront is the internal parasite. Nematodes, flukes, protozoa, and a host of other biological freeloaders often afflict imported snakes, lizards, turtles, tortoises, and amphibians. The most common parasite of bearded dragons is coccidia, which is very difficult to eliminate.

The good news is that because virtually all bearded dragons are captive bred they have normally not had the opportunity to pick up internal parasites. However, this does not completely exclude the possibility of a dragon picking up a parasitic infection. When housed in a filthy pet shop, wholesaler's, or private collection, even the healthiest of dragons can quickly succumb to a parasite infestation. By purchasing your animal from a reputable retailer or breeder and not allowing it contact with any other herps, you can go a long way in preventing internal parasites.

If you maintain several different species of herps, it is

Parasites are a common cause of unexplained weight loss in bearded dragons, but there are other possibilities as well.

Cryptosporidiosis

One dangerous internal parasite that cannot be cured is *Cryptosporidium,* sometimes known among herp hobbyists simply as "crypto." The infection itself is called cryptosporidiosis. Signs of crypto are similar to other parasitic infections and include vomiting, severe swelling and bloating, and rapid weight loss. Crypto is feared among hobbyists and commercial breeders because it can be present in an animal for two years or more before causing symptoms. Animals infected by crypto are doomed to die slowly and painfully and should be humanely euthanized.

especially important to quarantine new arrivals for at least a month prior to bringing them into the same room as the rest of your collection, lest a parasite load pass from one herp to the next. Reptile-specific parasites may also be passed from the dragon's food item into the dragon's system if the prey is infected. While anoles and house geckos can be offered as prey, the hobbyist must understand that any parasites that are in the anole or gecko may be passed on to the bearded dragon.

If you suspect that your dragon has contracted some variety of internal parasite, then an immediate trip to the vet is in order, as internal parasites are extremely dangerous and can seriously harm your dragon. Symptoms of parasite infection are highly variable and will be different based on the exact species of parasite afflicting your dragon. Some signs to look for include loss of appetite, listlessness, bloating, bloody or runny stool, vomiting, unexplained weight loss, discoloration and sinking of the eyes, sluggish movements, actually seeing worms in droppings, and constipation. Once diagnosed, the parasite can usually be dispatched by a prescribed regimen of oral or injected medicines.

External Parasites

Of course, not all parasites are internal. Mites, which are some of the most insidious and hated of all parasites, afflict the skin and eyes of the dragon. Mites are small. Measuring less than a few millimeters in diameter, mites appear as tiny, reddish, gray, or brownish black flecks crawling all over your lizard. By attaching themselves to the dragon with small, hooked legs and anchor-like mouthparts, mites bore through the skin of the dragon and suck minuscule amounts of its blood.

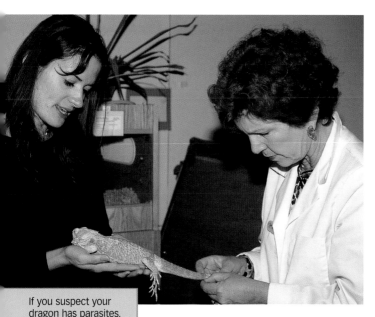

If you suspect your dragon has parasites, it is best to seek veterinary treatment rather than trying to fix the problem yourself.

Once gorged on blood, the mites release their hold on the afflicted lizard and lay eggs in the substrate and furnishings of the terrarium. Once the eggs hatch (and there will be thousands of them), the infestation will explode as a new generation of mites lays siege to your pet. Because mites are so prolific and almost always occur in large numbers, you'll need to diagnose and remedy the mite infestation quickly, for these loathsome arthropods can quickly drain your dragon of a significant amount of blood, reducing its appetite, weakening its immune system, and opening the flood gates for stress and secondary infection.

Break the cycle and destroy these vampiric attackers by using one or a combination of mite remedies. The least invasive and stressful method is to bathe the dragon and house it in quarantine while you clean the cage. In a shallow pan of clean, lukewarm water, bathe your dragon vigorously, paying special attention to the eyes, nostrils, vent, and the folds of skin and scales around the beard and neck, for all of these areas can shelter mites. No soap or cleanser is required in this bath. Once you've washed the lion's share of mites down the drain (making sure to curse each and every one of them as they swirl toward their watery graves), dry the dragon and place it in quarantine.

Pest Strips

Until recently, the standard mite treatment was to use vapona-impregnated insect-killing strips. However, more and more evidence is accumulating that these strips can cause death or injury in herps, sometimes many months after they have been used. It is probably best to avoid using them.

Scrub Brush for Beardies

When bathing your dragon to free it of mites, try scrubbing it with a soft, old toothbrush. As you gently massage the bristles of the toothbrush in the beard, between the scales, and all over the body of the dragon, you will be able to root out any clinging mites that otherwise might not have been washed off in the bath. Be sure to scrub gently.

Rid the home terrarium of mites by disposing of all substrate. Live plants must also be destroyed, as their pores, leaves, soil, and bark will all harbor mites. Any furnishings that can be thrown out should be. Place the disposable items in a plastic bag, tie it shut, and take it outdoors immediately to prevent mites from crawling out and finding their way back to your dragon. Décor that you wish to keep, such as large rocks, hunks of driftwood, and wooden perches, must be thoroughly cleansed of all mites and mite eggs. Wrap any items to be cleansed in aluminum foil and place them in your oven. Bake these items for two to three hours at 275°F (135°C). This temperature will not burn the décor, but it will destroy all mites hiding within the items.

Never bake any artificial items such as those made of glass, acrylic, or plastic. Artificial items must be washed in a chlorine bleach solution. Allow these items to soak in a weak (about 10 percent) bleach solution for at least an hour, but a full day is best. Wash them thoroughly afterward in hot water, making sure to rinse away any remaining bleach solution. Allow these items to dry and air out for several days before returning them to the terrarium.

Once you have cleaned all décor, you must now soak the terrarium itself in a bleach solution, for it is a guarantee that mites and mite eggs are hiding within the tiniest nooks and crannies of the tank. Wash the tank with the bleach solution and let it soak for 18 to 24 hours. Afterward, thoroughly rinse and air out the tank. It

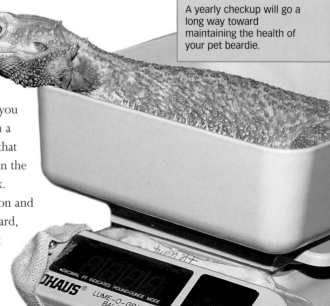

A yearly checkup will go a long way toward maintaining the health of your pet beardie.

is important that no chlorine bleach is left on the tank or any of its fixtures, as the vapors from this chemical can cause serious problems to your dragon.

Another method of mite removal is to dip the dragon in some type of cooking oil—vegetable, olive, soy, or the like. You want to dip the dragon in the oil completely and quickly; take it out immediately. Soak up the oil that remains on the beardie with a towel or rag. Then place the lizard in the quarantine tank and treat the cage as above. The oil method does stress the dragon somewhat and is not recommended for dragons under six months of age. Expect that dragon to shed its skin within a week or two of this treatment.

The third and final method of eradicating mites is to take the infested beardie to the veterinarian. The vet will prescribe a mite killer, most likely ivermectin. Usually, this medication is sprayed on the lizard and its cage. Ivemectin is toxic to turtles and tortoises, so if you keep these animals, be sure to never spray ivermectin near them or their enclosures.

Mite Treatment Reminder

Remember that mites lay eggs in the substrate and cage furnishings. You must treat the mites on the dragon as well as the mites and eggs that remain in the terrarium. Be prepared to repeat the treatment if some eggs survive the first one.

Infections
Mouth Rot

Technically known as infectious stomatitis, mouth rot is a bacterial infection that afflicts the mouth and gums of the dragon. Typically brought about by filthy living conditions and low temperatures, mouth rot almost never occurs in healthy dragons. Symptoms include bleeding from the gums, refusal to eat, a blackening of the teeth, swelling inside the mouth, and the accumulation of a cheesy, yellowish exudate between the teeth.

If left unchecked, mouth rot will ultimately prove fatal. Mouth rot causes the dragon extreme pain and must be treated as soon as it is discovered. If caught in a late stage, the disease will be considerably more difficult to treat and may even lead to permanent facial disfigurement. Seek veterinary care immediately. Prevent future attacks of mouth rot by maintaining clean environs and offering ample heat to your dragon. There is some speculation that mouth rot results from insufficient vitamin C in the diet. To ensure your dragon gets enough vitamin C, gut-load the feeder insects and offer a wide variety of fresh vegetables.

Abscess

An abscess occurs when a burn, cut, scrape, or abrasion is poorly treated and allowed to become infected. Within the old wound (though under the skin), there will form a pustule, or sphere of pus. Pus is naturally produced by most vertebrate animals as a means of flushing out wounds and fighting infection. In the case of the abscess, however, the pus remains within the body and, because it is unable to flow out, will become heavily infected with bacteria. If left unchecked, the pustule will either burst and flow back into the body (thereby poisoning the blood and making your dragon very sick), or it will dry up, harden, and become a painful, tumor-like lump under the skin.

Once an abscess is noticed, take your pet to the vet. Your veterinarian will puncture and drain the abscess, suture it, and usually prescribe a regimen of antibiotics to combat further infection.

The inside of a dragon's mouth is normally a little yellowish; do not confuse this with the yellow crust of mouth rot.

Respiratory Infection

Respiratory illnesses in bearded dragons are uncommon, and most often occur as a bacterial infection of the respiratory tract immediately following a bad bout with mouth rot. Respiratory infections may also be caused by excessively cold or damp conditions within the bearded dragon's terrarium. Prolonged exposure to high levels of relative humidity is another culprit of this malady. A respiratory infection causes labored breathing, hissing or huffing sounds that accompany the breathing, holding the mouth agape, build-up of crust or dried mucus around the nostrils and corners of the mouth, bubbles forming in the nostrils, and excessive production of saliva.

Treat a respiratory infection by taking your dragon to the veterinarian ASAP. He or she will diagnose the problem and treat it with a medical regimen. As for your end of the bargain, make sure to correct any offending conditions in the bearded dragon's enclosure: raise ambient temperatures, create a basking spot, increase ventilation, decrease relative humidity, and maintain scrupulously clean environs, making sure to remove any feces, urine, and other wastes as soon as they occur.

Metabolic Bone Disease

Perhaps the most tragic of bearded dragon ailments, metabolic bone disease (known as MBD) is a slow, debilitating, and painful ailment that is brought about by inadequate exposure to ultraviolet light, which causes a deficiency of vitamin D3. Only by soaking up the UVB rays of either natural, unfiltered sunlight or by basking under the artificial UVB light cast by a special light bulb can bearded dragons adequately metabolize calcium and synthesize vitamin D3 into strong bones and healthy teeth. Without this UVB exposure, the dragon develops weak, crooked, and poorly calcified bones. The result is a frail and often disfigured dragon whose bones are susceptible to fracture and breakage. Once diagnosed, MBD is treatable only based on how advanced it is. In its early stages, the disease may be reversed by increased exposure to UV rays and increased vitamin D3 and calcium supplementation. If MBD is too advanced, however, the

The kinked tail of this orange beardie could be evidence that it had metabolic bone disease in the past.

Spic and Span

Most infectious diseases in bearded dragons stem from filthy living conditions. Unsanitary housing leads to increased stress levels, suppressed immune systems, and increased pathogen numbers. Maintain a clean enclosure by removing all droppings as soon as possible, keeping a supply of clean, fresh water at your dragon's disposal at all times, and conducting regular and thorough cleanings of the entire terrarium. Warm, clean, and dry living conditions are a hobbyist's first line of defense against diseases and disorders in their bearded dragons.

damage is irreversible and the lizard will be forever disfigured. The most severe cases require the humane euthanasia of the dragon.

It's so sad to see a dragon that must limp or drag behind its gnarled legs, or one that must crawl slowly or awkwardly because it has a twisted spine or curled hips. Misaligned jaws and

- **Jaws soft and bent outward.**
- **Dragon has trouble walking.**
- **Backbone, pelvis, tail, and/or limbs are crooked or bent.**
- **Thighs are swollen and hard to the touch.**
- **Unexplained limb fractures.**
- **Dragon trembles or convulses (occurs after the other signs).**

improperly formed skulls also hallmark this tragic ailment. The saddest thing about MBD, however, is that it is 100 percent preventable. The hobbyist has only to care for his or her dragon properly, offering ample UV radiation, nutritious diet, and proper vitamin supplementation. When these conditions are met, MBD will virtually never strike. As you might imagine, ample UVB exposure and calcium/vitamin D3 supplementation is most critical during the earliest stages of the dragon's life.

Vitamin Toxicity

Vitamin toxicity occurs when one type of vitamin or another builds up in the animal's body to an excessive level. Symptoms include bloating, jerky or skittish behavior, confusion, loss of appetite, loss of color, and, in extreme cases, death. The most common form of vitamin toxicity comes from high intakes of vitamin A. Bearded dragons are very slow to metabolize and use vitamin A, and regular dosages of this vitamin (frequently found in vitamin supplement powders) can soon result in an unhealthy stockpile of vitamin A in the dragon's body. Alleviate this problem by offering only vitamin supplements that contain beta carotene instead of vitamin A. The dragon's digestive system will metabolize the beta carotene into a basic form of vitamin A when it needs that nutrient, but it will pass out any excess beta carotene without incident, thereby bypassing the problem of toxicity altogether.

To avoid other forms of vitamin toxicity, do not give your dragons supplementation more often than is recommended. If your beardie is housed outdoors, it is best not to supplement vitamin D3 at all to prevent vitamin D toxicity.

Egg Binding

A disorder that occasionally strikes a bearded dragon is egg binding, or dystocia. Dystocia occurs when a gravid (pregnant) female cannot or will not rid her body of all the eggs she is carrying. This is typically due to the unavailability of suitable nesting sites. If no suitable nesting sites are available, a female beardie may carry her eggs too long. During this exaggerated gestation, the eggs may grow too large for the female to pass them, thus the female may well carry the eggs inside her until she dies.

Symptoms of egg binding include swelling around the mid-body, unwillingness to deposit the eggs (prolonged gestation), and continual, anxious movement (often including digging) around the terrarium. In such cases, the remedy to the problem may simply be to provide the female with suitable nesting sites (see Chapter 7). If this is the problem, you can expect the female to deposit her brood within hours (if not minutes) of finding a suitable laying place. If the female still does not lay her eggs, the problem may have another cause and will be considerably more difficult to correct.

Sometimes a large or oddly shaped egg will get lodged in the female's reproductive tract. This egg blocks all the eggs behind it. In other cases, an egg may die in utero, and it will begin to decompose inside the female's body. The rotting egg causes the female dragon's immune system to go on the offensive, thereby causing swelling throughout the reproductive tract. If the female had MBD in the past, her pelvis could be misshapen and prevent the eggs from passing out of her body. If any of these scenarios are the case, you must get your bearded dragon to a veterinarian immediately for X rays and surgical treatment. Untreated dystocia is excruciatingly painful, and it can turn fatal in a matter of days.

Help prevent dystocia by frequently handling and exercising your female bearded dragon, especially in the months before pre-breeding conditioning occurs. A strong, muscular female is far less likely to have problems with egg binding. Weak, sluggish, underweight, or underexercised females are much more prone to egg binding, as are those that received too little calcium and/or vitamin D3 in the pre-breeding conditioning period.

Obesity

Wild bearded dragons are active all day long and their food sources are often scant, thus, their metabolism and constitution have evolved such that these lizards may survive on small rations. In captivity, however, a great many dragons will exist under the exact opposite conditions—too much to eat and too little activity. The result is an obese and unhealthy reptilian lump. Signs of obesity include listlessness, sluggishness, slow movements, labored breathing, and a generally fat appearance. Obesity leads to myriad health problems and even death from heart failure. Combat obesity by replacing most animal fare with vegetable matter and taking your dragon out for regular exercise.

This female dragon is digging a nest. Lack of a proper nesting site is the most common cause of egg binding.

Provide your female dragon with a suitable nesting site sooner rather than later.

Supportive Care

No matter what sort of affliction your dragon has, there are certain measures you can take to help ensure that your pet's recovery is as fast and as problem-free as possible. Once your veterinarian has diagnosed the problem and has begun a treatment regimen, make sure you stick to the prescribed dosages and treatments. Very often a vet will give a preliminary injection of antibiotic or some other drug to begin the healing process, and then he or she will send you home with a prescription for your dragon. Sticking to that prescription and faithfully following the doctor's orders to the letter are the best things you could do for your ailing dragon. If, for example, the vet says to give a medicine for 14 days, but your dragon seems well after only 11 days, it would be unwise of you to end treatment three days early.

Turn Up the Heat

Like all reptiles, bearded dragons are ectothermic, and their metabolism and other bodily processes are contingent on the temperature of their surroundings. Raise the ambient temperature in the dragon's enclosure by three to five degress, and do not allow the temperature to drop during the night. Raising the temperature in the basking spot is also advisable; maintain a basking spot of 102°-105°F (38.9° to 40.6°C). This extra heat will enable your dragon's immune system to work at peak efficiency and will help it to fight off infection.

Vital Food

An enhanced diet is also in order. Add additional vitamin and mineral supplements to meal (do not add extra vitamin A) per week, and make sure each insect meal has been gut-loaded before offering it to the dragon. Because the dragon's body needs all the nutrients it can get, you'll want to offer your ailing dragon just as much food as it will eat, paying special attention to the dark green and deep red vegetables, both of which are a great source of vitamins and antioxidants. If your dragon is suffering from a vitamin toxicity, follow your veterinarian's diet recommendations.

If your dragon is not eating because of its illness (as is often the case with some varieties of internal parasite or advanced cases of mouth rot), then your veterinarian may prescribe some fluids or liquid foods, which you may have to force-feed to your dragon. Force-feeding isn't always easy, and it isn't something that a newcomer to the hobby should attempt with a blind eye. Get your veterinarian or another skilled expert to instruct you in this area before you attempt it. Only force-feed if told to do so by a veterinarian.

Signs of an Unhealthy Dragon

If your beardie displays any of the signs in the list below, it may need veterinary attention. If you are in doubt, it is better to seek the opinion of a veterinarian with experience in reptile medicine than to wait and see what happens. The sooner the animal sees the vet, the greater the chance it will recover.

- Abnormal feces—runny, odd color, excessive odor, worms
- Inability to right itself when turned upside down
- Limping or dragging a limb
- Listless or sluggish behavior—can be caused by cool temperatures
- Refusing food—can be caused by temperature extremes
- Sunken eyes
- Vomiting
- Weight loss

Chapter 7

Captive Breeding

Considered by many hobbyists to be the high-water mark of any herp endeavor, the breeding of a pet reptile can be a rewarding and uniquely fulfilling experience. It's a chance for the hobbyist to both witness the miracle of life and to watch his or her own pet progress through all the stages of its own life, from newborn, to adult, to parent. But captive breeding is not a matter to be taken lightly or conducted on a whim. Propagation forces the conscientious hobbyist to ask some very frank questions: Are my animals in peak health and can they withstand the rigors of breeding? Do I have the facilities to incubate the eggs once my female deposits them? What will I do with the young (sometimes over two dozen of them) once they hatch? Can I adequately house, heat, and feed the young until I sell them or give them to other responsible keepers? The hobbyist must answer these questions in a realistic and reasonable manner before he or she can decide to go ahead and breed their bearded dragons.

Don't Let This Happen to You

When I was in college, I had a "pair" of dragons that just wouldn't mate. I'd done everything right. My dragons were in peak health, it was the right time of year, I had an incubator that was just waiting to receive the eggs, but my lizards simply wouldn't mate. Then a friend of mine came over and I told her my problem. She lifted each dragon out of its terrarium, inspected the cloaca, and laughed. "Unless you plan on cultivating the first female-female spawning, I suggest you invest in a male beardie!" I flushed red at my blunder and bought a male dragon later that month.

Sexing

First and foremost, you must obtain two dragons of the opposite sex. Sexing an adult dragon is relatively easy to do. Lift your adult dragon from its enclosure and inspect its vent or cloacal opening. Males of the species will have enlarged femoral pores lining the underside of the hind legs, enlarged preanal scales (usually six of them) about half an inch anterior to the cloaca, a wide cloacal opening, and two noticeable bulges on either side of the vent—these bulges being the hemipenes (the paired copulatory organs) tucked away in their pouches. Sexually active males will also display an enlarged beard, which usually turns a dark brown to black or bluish during the mating season. Additionally, males have wider heads than females, reach a larger size, and are more robust overall.

Females, on the other hand, have much smaller femoral pores and preanal scales, the opening of the cloaca will be considerably narrower, and there will be no hemipenal bulges along the sides of the cloaca. Adult female dragons also grow to be considerably shorter than their male counterparts, and their heads are correspondingly slimmer about the jaws. If you have a chance to inspect several adult specimens in conjunction with one another, the differences between the sexes should become readily apparent.

Until the animals are sexually mature, the sexes are difficult to distinguish. There is a method to sex hatchlings and juveniles, but the differences between the sexes are still subtle and it takes practice to accurately determine the sex. The method involves putting the dragon on a flat surface with the tail pointing at you. Gently lift the tail up and over the back of the dragon. Stop when you meet any resistance, as you do not want to injure the beardie's tail. When you feel resistance, gently and slowly roll the tail back and forth

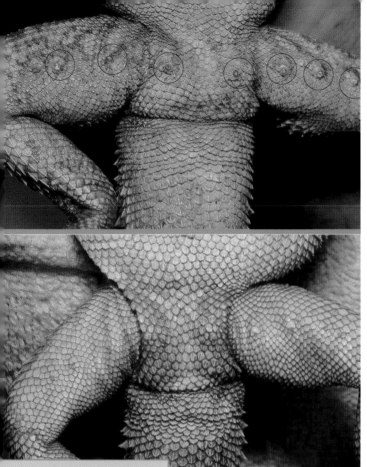

You can determine the sex of adult bearded dragons by looking at the pores on the undersides of the thighs. Males (top) have larger and more numerous pores than do females.

between your fingers while looking at the underside of the tail near the base. If, as you roll the tail, a slight depression appears in the middle, the beardie is probably male. If no depression appears, the beardie is probably female. The depression is the space between the two hemipenes. Modern technology can also lend a hand in sex determination, as DNA tests and X rays (which can be conducted by most veterinarians) are all but foolproof in determining the sex of even a young dragon.

Age

Once you've obtained a definite sexual pair of dragons, the next question is one of age. At what age are bearded dragons capable of copulation? At the age of 24 to 28 months, bearded dragons become sexually mature, and females stay fertile through about five to six years old. Older males, however, retain the ability to impregnate females throughout their entire adult life.

Now just because a female dragon *can* produce young at this age, it doesn't mean that she *should* be bred at this age. Females who breed at their youngest possible age of two years produce smaller clutches, fewer clutches, and lose their reproductive viability at an earlier age. Females who do not breed until their third year of life, on the other hand, tend to produce larger clutches, more clutches, and they remain reproductively viable for a

Sperm Retention

As in many reptiles, female beardies can retain sperm within their bodies for some time. This allows them to produce viable eggs long after an encounter with a male. Therefore, don't be surprised if a lone female produces several more clutches without reintroducing the male.

considerably longer period of time. One of my females—an old gal I'd affectionately dubbed as "Haggard Hazel"—was still producing clutches at the ripe old age of eight years, and I've heard rumors of females still breeding at over nine years old.

Though other breeders may disagree, I feel that a female should not be bred in captivity until she is at least 32 to 36 months old, as breeding her earlier will result in her producing far fewer offspring over the course of her productive years. Males, once they've matured past 24 months old, may be bred for the rest of their lives without any negative side effects.

Pre-Breeding Conditioning

Perhaps the most critical step in a beardie breeding project is the pre-breeding conditioning phase. Pre-breeding conditioning is the act of preparing your lizards as best you can for the upcoming breeding season. Though we might not think it, breeding takes a toll on both lizards, but especially on the female, for the formation of the eggs, the gestation period, and the deposition of the eggs is a taxing period, so you'll want your dragon-girl to be in peak condition before mating.

Begin pre-breeding conditioning in the fall, around November. Supply each and every meal you give your dragons with additional calcium/D3 supplements. The female will need all the calcium she can get, so that the upcoming formation of eggs within her body will progress

Bearded dragons must be in peak condition before you attempt to breed them.

normally. Females that are lacking in calcium will produce flawed, thin-shelled, or otherwise inferior eggs that stand a limited chance of hatching. Excess calcium will not harm the female, and it will go a long way in ensuring that her eggs are thick-shelled and healthy when she deposits them.

Brumation

The next step is to hibernate your dragons; the more correct term is actually *brumate*, an incomplete state of hibernation. In the wild, bearded dragons brumate or become dormant for at least a few weeks out of the year when the weather becomes cool. This period of cool temperatures and reduced activity followed by warming and a return to normal activity causes the formation and release of reproductive hormones. These hormones are a biological signal to the reptile that "it's time to find a mate and spread my genes!"

In captivity, this natural period of inactivity can easily be simulated.

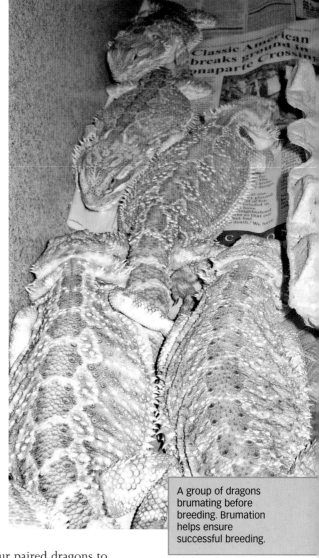

A group of dragons brumating before breeding. Brumation helps ensure successful breeding.

Begin around December by removing your paired dragons to separate enclosures (if they were living in one tank) so that they cannot even see one another. Gradually (over a period of 10 days to two weeks) lower the temperature in each terrarium to a daily range of 75° to 80°F (23.9° to 26.7°C) with nightly dips ranging from 62° to 70°F (16.7° to 21.1°C). Reduce the amount of light each terrarium receives to 7 to 9 hours each day. If at all possible (by way of a dehumidifier, perhaps), lower the relative humidity in the dragons' enclosure to 25 to 30 percent, as this increased dryness will closely simulate the natural climatic cycles of Australia and will help trigger healthy hormonal production.

You'll soon notice that your dragons' activity level has fallen dramatically. They will seldom eat and may remain in hiding for days at the time, though basking may still occur. You will find your dragons will eat much less food or abstain from eating altogether. Offer food only once or twice a week, but keep a supply of clean, fresh water at your lizards' disposal at all times.

Allow your dragons to remain in this semi-hibernation state for 10 to 12 weeks. Then, around the end of March or the beginning of April, begin slowly raising the temperatures and increasing the photoperiod (amount of daylight) each day until temperatures have returned to normal and resume 10 to 14 hours of lighting daily. Once their activity begins to pick up, you'll want to feed each dragon as much food as it will take, making sure to apply added calcium to each of the female's meals. I also recommend feeding the female a couple of juvenile mice (called *fuzzies* or *hoppers* depending on the size) or small lizards (anoles or house geckos) during this time, as the minerals and proteins in the mice or lizards will help to optimize the female's ability to produce a healthy clutch. Feed them in this manner for 10 to 12 days.

Bad Boys

Occasionally, a male bearded dragon may be overly aggressive with the female and bite too hard, causing serious bleeding. Aggressive males may also bite off the toes, tip of the tail, and even the tip of the snout of the females. While this behavior is typically prevalent when older males are bred with younger females, it may occur between any dragon couple. Keep a close eye on your dragons for the first few hours once copulation has begun. If the male appears overly aggressive, remove him to another enclosure.

Mating

When you introduce the two animals, be sure to *place the male in the female's enclosure*, not the other way around. It is important for your female to be as comfortable and secure as possible during the mating process, so allowing her to remain in the familiar environs of her terrarium will help to ease her stress and promote a fruitful copulation. While some hobbyists may not have a preference as to which dragon is introduced into which terrarium, I find that copulation and mating occur more smoothly and with less incident when the male

Selective breeding of bearded dragons has led to the development of color varieties. A yellow dragon is pictured.

is placed in the female's enclosure.

When the female is placed in the male's enclosure, the male tends to be rougher with the female and overly aggressive. To him, it seems that she is intruding into his territory, thus he is more aggressive. By placing the male in the female's enclosure, the male is out of his comfort zone and tends to display less aggressive and territorial behaviors during the mating process.

When you place the male in the female's enclosure, he will not take long in declaring his intentions. The male will sniff the ground and taste the substrate, vigorously bob his head in sight of the female, and puff out his bristly beard, which by now may have taken on a leaden gray to black or bluish hue. In response to his advances, the female may roam about the cage with the male in hot pursuit, or she may engage in arm-waving, indicating that she is ready to mate.

The male will close in on the female from behind or from the side, bite her firmly on the jaws or the nape of the neck, and wrap his forelimbs around her upper body. While he has her in his jaws, the male may drag the female around the terrarium or shake her violently. While this behavior may look aggressive, it is actually quite necessary for successful copulation. Younger males that do not overpower their older female mates are sometimes snubbed by the females, while older, skillfully dominant males have no such troubles.

When he is ready, the male will tilt the female's rear portions with his hind legs and tail, expose her cloaca, and insert one of his hemipenes. The dragons may remain locked in this

Nesting Testing

Female bearded dragons may dig several "phantom holes" in the laying substrate before actually depositing their eggs. Digging one false hole after another may simply be the result of the female's being finicky about where she lays her eggs, or it may be an instinctual tactic designed to confuse would-be predators so that, in the wild, the real nest containing the eggs might be overlooked by a prowling monitor lizard. Whatever the reason, expect your female beardie to dig several false holes before she lays her brood.

posture for only a few seconds or as long as several minutes. Expect your dragons to repeat these behaviors numerous times throughout the day and night. If you have multiple female dragons, you can simply move the male from one of their enclosures to the next so that he will breed with each one of them. After a period of about five to seven days of sporadic copulation, the chances that your female is successfully fertilized are very good.

Remove the male and put him back into his own enclosure and continue to offer increased quantities of nutritious food, with an increased calcium dosage and slightly increased vitamin dosage going to the female. Feed the female plenty of food with as wide a variety as you can so that her developing brood will be as healthy as possible.

Gravidity and Nesting

If the mating was successful, the female will be gravid (pregnant with eggs) and start showing signs of this within a month or a little less. When a month has passed, you'll notice that the female has taken on a swollen, bulky appearance. This is due to the developing eggs inside her, which may number from as few as 8 to 10 or as many as 22 to 26, depending on the size of the female. As the eggs grow larger and larger, the female may stop eating. This is normal and is one more reason why it is so important the she be well fed up to this point.

Soon after you notice her bulging belly, you'll also notice an increased level of activity: roaming the terrarium, clawing at the glass, and excessive digging. These are all key indicators that she is ready to deposit her eggs, and you must supply her with a suitable spot in which to do so. If deprived of a suitable nesting site, the female will either deposit her eggs in the dry substrate of her terrarium (where the eggs will quickly dehydrate and die), deposit them in the water bowl (where they will drown), or retain the eggs and suffer from dystocia, also known as "egg binding." Dystocia is a very serious problem that will ultimately be fatal for both the eggs and the female. I recommend establishing a nesting or laying box sooner rather than later. Having suitable media available before the female is ready to lay is certainly preferable to forcing the female to suffer and wait for you to finally offer her a suitable laying site.

The good news is that constructing a suitable nesting site is cheaper and easier than you might think. Many hobbyists—myself included—use a plastic sweater box

Slugs

Occasionally, a female dragon will drop an unfertilized egg. Known as a dud or a slug, these infertile eggs are easily recognizable. They are smaller than their fertile counterparts and are typically a translucent tan or tea color, owing to their poor calcification and lifelessness. If allowed to incubate with the rest of the clutch, the slug will soon begin to rot and will jeopardize the entire clutch by spreading mold and bacteria to the rest of the eggs. Remove and dispose of any slugs as soon as you notice them.

filled with moist vermiculite, which may be obtained from any hardware story, garden center, or plant nursery.

Moist, in this case, means spongy and not dripping wet. A good formula for mixing egg-depositing substrate is to mix two parts vermiculite to one part water based on weight, not on volume. Other good egg-laying substrates include moistened perlite, sphagnum moss, or fine-grained sand. In all cases, you want the laying substrate just moist enough to hold together when you dig in it. After layering the moist vermiculite to at least

Sand makes a suitable medium for the nesting box.

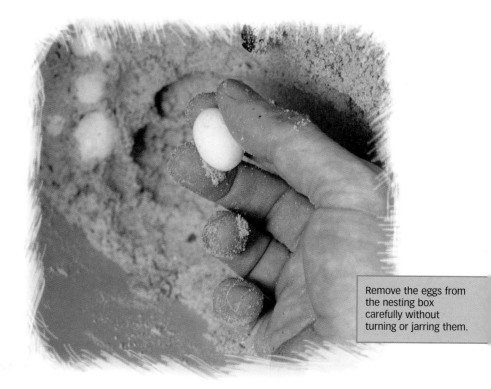

Remove the eggs from the nesting box carefully without turning or jarring them.

three to four inches deep, cut a large hole in the side of the box and put the lid on the top. Place the box inside the female's terrarium. When she is ready to deposit her eggs, the female will crawl into the box through the hole cut in the side, dig a flask-shaped hole (typically in the corner of the box) in the moist vermiculite, and back her rear portions into or directly above the hole. She will then being the long, laborious process of depositing her clutch, an event that may last for several hours, depending on the size of the clutch and the size of the individual eggs.

Of course, the sweater-box method is not the only way of building a laying box. Cat litter trays, storage bins, small (clean) garbage cans, and even other modified terraria may be used. As long as the box provides the female with adequately damp substrate and gives her enough privacy so that she can lay her eggs in peace, almost any container will suffice. In the wild, the female is extremely vulnerable to attack by predators while she is laying her eggs, and she knows it. In captivity, this instinct will make the female very uncomfortable if she is not adequately sheltered during egg laying. I advise leaving the room while she lays, as well as covering the entire terrarium with towels so as to afford the female as much privacy as possible.

Check on the female periodically, and once she has left the laying box, you can remove it and place the eggs in your incubator. Before leaving the laying box, however, the female dragon will have covered up her eggs so thoroughly it may be difficult to determine just exactly where they are buried. Gently and carefully move aside the vermiculite until you find the clutch. The eggs will be very delicate, so great care must be taken when removing them. Do not bump, turn, rotate, or otherwise jar the eggs as you move them, as this can kill the dragon embryo inside. If two or more eggs have adhered together, do not separate them, as this will break or severely weaken the shells and can ultimately lead to the death of the eggs.

Once you've removed all the eggs from the laying box and placed them in your incubator, you should turn your attentions back to the female. Likely to be thin, worn, and tired, the female should be allowed to hide quietly away in a dark retreat for the next day or so while she recovers. Feed her a few more protein-rich meals and offer her plenty of water, as egg laying radically lowers a dragon's hydration level. A week after laying her eggs, the female can return to her normal dietary regimen.

Incubation Reminder

Temperature fluctuations inside the incubator can cause the embryonic dragons serious problems. Most often, clutches that have been subjected to wide temperature variations will produce a high number of deformed hatchlings. Keep temperatures inside the incubator as constant as possible.

Incubation

When it comes to an incubator, it is highly advisable to have this item set up and running well before the female lays her eggs. That way you can simply and easily transplant the eggs from the laying box to the incubator, which will already be functioning at a stable temperature and humidity. When you first set up the incubator, temperatures can fluctuate widely, which is very detrimental to the eggs.

Incubator Construction

A good incubator may be built from commercially available quail and chicken egg incubators, or a homemade version can be constructed using a Styrofoam cooler, two bricks, a small plastic storage box, and a fully submersible aquarium heater. A thermometer, particularly a digital one that stores high and low temperatures, will be very helpful.

Begin construction by placing the two bricks, laying on their sides, in the bottom of the Styrofoam cooler. Between the bricks, place the aquarium heater. Fill the cooler with water until the level is just below the top of the bricks. Punch a series of small holes in the lid and bottom of the plastic storage box. Atop the bricks, place the plastic storage box. Put an inch or two of moist vermiculite or a thick layer of moist paper towels in the bottom of the storage box. Lay the eggs atop this layer inside the storage box. Put the lid on the storage box. Turn the aquarium heater on and set at 86°F (30°C). Place the lid on the cooler.

The heater will both heat the air in the cooler, and it will cause water to evaporate from the pool in the bottom of the cooler. The water will all but saturate the atmosphere inside the cooler, and the holes you punched in the lid of the plastic container will allow water vapor to enter the storage container and reach the eggs. The holes that you punched in the bottom of the storage container will allow all excess water to drip back into the reservoir in the bottom of the cooler. There are many variations on this general design that are all very successful, and there are many great (and not too expensive) herp specific incubators for sale through pet shops, online, and as advertised in herp magazines.

Incubation Temperatures and Humidity

Proper incubation of bearded dragon eggs should consist of temperatures ranging from 82° to 86°F (27.8° to 30°C). Maintain a stable temperature inside the incubator, with as little fluctuation as possible, for even a very short-lived spike or drop in temperature can

A Box for Each Clutch

If you breed multiple female bearded dragons, do not mix their clutches in the same incubation box. If one clutch begins hatching before the other clutch does, then the embryonic fluid from the eggs in the first clutch will contaminate the incubation media in which the second clutch still sits. The media will be loaded with rotting embryonic fluids, and serious bacterial and fungal growth will occur. For this reason, never mix clutches that were deposited more than a couple of days apart.

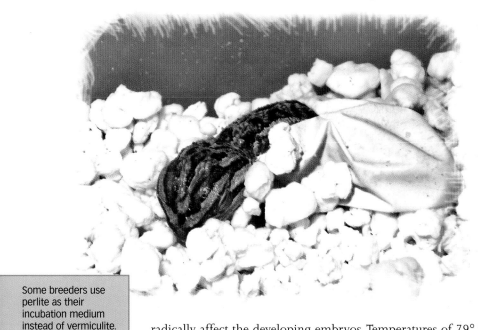

radically affect the developing embryos. Temperatures of 79° to 82°F (26.1° to 27.8°C) will result in slower development of the eggs but a more gentle disposition in the emerging dragons, while temperatures under 78°F (25.6°C) will likely result in the death of the eggs. Conversely, temperatures of 86° to 88°F (30° to 31.1°C) will result in a quicker hatch time and the emerging young are prone to displaying more flighty and even semi-aggressive behaviors. Temperatures exceeding 89°F (31.7°C) will often result in deformity or death of the developing embryos.

Relative humidity is also a major factor in the successful incubation of the eggs. Maintain relative humidity at 75 to 85 percent. Anything higher or lower, and the eggs will either dehydrate or canker, respectively. You'll also want to keep an eye out for any molds or fungus that might develop on the eggshells. If this occurs, simply wipe off the offending mold with a damp rag and, if at all possible, isolate the moldy egg to the corner of the incubator. Do not throw away an egg on which mold occasionally grows, for it may be alive and well. I've had many mold-growing eggs hatch into beautiful baby beardies.

Hatching

After a period of 55 to 85 days—depending on the temperature at which you incubate them—you can expect your eggs to begin hatching. The first stage of the hatch, known as

Hatchlings and Humidity

Hatchling bearded dragons are born with thin skin, and they have a higher surface-area to body-mass ratio than adults. Both of these qualities mean that the baby dragons run a high risk of dehydration. Keeping multiple water dishes available in the baby dragons' enclosure, giving weekly baths, feeding plenty of moist or juicy foods, and maintaining a higher relative humidity (perhaps through spraying lightly with a plant mister) inside the enclosure will all help to prevent the hatchling dragons from dehydrating.

pipping, occurs when the neonatal lizards slash open their shells, but do not emerge. Lasting anywhere from a few hours to a few days, the pipping period is that time in which the baby dragon rests inside its partially opened shell and absorbs the last of its yolk sac and starts breathing air. It is critical that you not tamper with the pipping dragons or try to force them out of their shells; they will come out when they are ready. Keeping a lid on the cooler is mandatory during the pipping stage, for if the hobbyist continually removes this lid to watch the young hatch, the air inside the incubator will drastically drop in humidity. This can cause the eggshells to harden and constrict the hatching lizards. Second, the inner storage box must be securely lidded, for when the baby dragons emerge, they will soon begin to wander and explore. Should one climb out of the inner storage box and fall into the water reservoir beneath, it could easily drown.

A final word on the incubation of the eggs is that all the eggs may not hatch at the same time. While most clutches hatch entirely within a few days (the last egg in the clutch hatching within 72 hours of the first), the occasional clutch may sport one or more late bloomers. I've had dragon eggs hatch nearly two weeks after the rest of the brood has emerged, so don't throw out any unhatched eggs simply because the young has not emerged yet. Not until the egg has puckered, shriveled, or begun to rot should you throw it away.

Raising the Young

Once all the eggs have hatched, you should construct a home for all the new arrivals, preferably a few days before the young hatch. For the first couple of weeks of life, I recommend housing the hatchling dragons in 10-gallon (37.9 l) terraria at a density of no more than five dragons per terrarium. You don't want to overcrowd these delicate little lizards. Floor the terrarium with a thick layer of soft, white, unscented paper towels. These

This dragon has lost a leg to hungry siblings. Be sure to feed your babies enough food.

towels must be totally free of inks and perfumes, which can adversely affect the developing dragons. I advise against using sand or other coarse substrates, for the site on each young dragon's belly at which the yolk was attached will take up to two weeks to completely close, and sand or other abrasive material can irritate this sensitive spot. Maintain ambient temperatures of 80° to 84°F (26.7° to 28.9°C) with a basking spot of 92° to 100°F (33.3° to 37.8°C). The hatchlings will be able to withstand a drop in the temperature at night, just as the adults can. Feed the young dragons fruit flies, pinhead crickets, one-quarter-size crickets, and other such tiny insects.

Well, if you've gotten to this point, congratulations are in order, for you are now a proud parent (well, sort of) of a bunch of bouncing, baby bearded dragons! Make sure to separate the dragons within two to three weeks of hatching, as they will grow fast and territoriality between brother and sister hatchlings will soon rise, possibly resulting in nipped tails and bitten-off toes.

A far more common problem that arises with nipped tails and bitten-off toes comes not from territoriality, but from hunger. Baby beardies have very high metabolic rates and need to consume several small meals a day. When their nutritional needs are not being met (e.g., the hobbyist feeding them too infrequently), the young will look to any organic item available for food. When this occurs, the tankmates suffer nipped toes, lost tails, and, in severe cases, lost limbs or even death due to mauling. Curb this cannibalism by keeping a supply of fresh vegetables at your dragons' disposal at all times. Finely shredded or chopped, these veggies should keep even the most ravenous beardie from munching on his brethren between insect feedings.

Selective Breeding and Color Varieties

As is the case with most frequently bred reptiles and amphibians in the pet trade, bearded dragons are quite often the subjects of selective breeding projects. By breeding only those individuals that display the desired traits (i.e., bright color, large size, or what have you), the resulting brood is most likely to express *even more* of those desired traits. So a pair of beardies that seem to have a little more yellow around the jaws are bred, and their offspring display still a little more yellow, then that generation's offspring are even more yellow, and so on and so on until you have a generation of hatchling dragons that display almost total yellow body coloration. Of course, actual selective breeding isn't quite that simple, for you cannot simply breed brother and sister animals without winnowing down the gene pool and amplifying defects and heinous genetic deformities. Selective breeding of bearded dragons is definitely for the more advanced hobbyist who has a solid working knowledge of breeding and genetics under his or her belt.

The rest of us can still profit from the selective breeding projects of those experts in the form of new and stunning varieties of bearded dragon. Even as I write this text, new forms of beardies are being conceived in the minds of professional breeders, and by the time this book goes to press, hits the shelves of retail book stores, and winds up in your hands, the color varieties I mention here may have become old hat. New varieties of bearded dragon literally appear every breeding season.

The intensely colored Sandfire dragon is one of the best known and most sought after color varieties.

Sandfire Dragons

One of the first genetically manipulated bearded dragons appeared in the early 1990s and was dubbed the "Sandfire" dragon, which was selectively bred from those dragons that displayed the most orange and red in their natural coloration.

This strain took its name from Sandfire Dragon Ranch, where it was first produced by owner and herpetoculturist Bob Mailloux. The offspring of these dragons either displayed some reddish or orange coloration, or they merely carried the genes for those colors, but displayed only their standard tan/brown coloration. Over the years, the red/orange coloration in these lizards has become so vibrant that it's getting hard to look at one without wearing sunglasses! The Sandfire line has divided into several strains that refer to their predominant color. Sandfire dragons that are mostly crimson and fire-red are called Sandfire reds, while those that are rich yellow and mustard golden are called Sandfire golds.

Look at the Parents

In most color varieties of bearded dragon, the hatchlings do not appear very different from normal hatchlings, the color developing only when the dragon is a few months old. Furthermore, there are great variations in how well individuals express the specific color. The best predictor of how colorful a baby dragon will become is the color of the parents. If possible, ask to see the parents of a hatchling beardie you may purchase to get a good idea how colorful it will become.

Gold Dragons

Another color strain to emerge in the 1990s was the gold dragon. Bred from those wild dragons that displayed both red and golden hues, these animals probably share some genetics with the Sandfire line. Particularly stunning individuals look very much as if they were cast from solid gold, especially about the head and limbs. When adult males enter the breeding season, they take on an especially regal appearance, for their dark black to blue beards are offset nicely against their golden base coloration.

It is nearly impossible to determine how colorful a hatchling will become as it grows. This is a hatchling Sandfire gold dragon.

Lemon-Fire

The lemon-fire dragons represent a sort of mixture between the vibrant red of the Sandfire dragon and the crisp gold of the gold dragon. Wearing a base coat of bright yellow that is accented about the head, jaws, and flanks with crimson, these dragons are truly a sight to behold. So bright, in fact, are some of these dragons, that a fellow herp enthusiast remarked that they appeared to be radioactive.

Blood-Red

One of the darkest bearded dragons I've ever seen for sale is the blood-red (sometimes called ruby-red). This strain of dragon was created by the breeding of only the reddest of the red dragons, and it truly looks as if it is drenched in fresh blood.

Pale Varieties

Of course, not all hobbyists like these vibrantly colored red, yellow, and golden animals. Fortunately for them, the world of the enhanced bearded dragon has some other selections. Take, for example, the leucistic dragon. Having lost virtually all of its darker pigmentation, the leucistic dragon is almost completely white. Not to be mistaken for an albino (an animal that has no pigment), the leucistic dragon sports ivory pigmentation that makes it look almost like a ghost. True albino dragons also exist, as do the so-called snow dragons that exhibit a similar, all-white coloration as the leucistic dragons.

German Giants

Of course, color isn't the only quality for which bearded dragons are selectively bred. Size is also a major area of specialization. The German giant bearded dragon comes from a stock of naturally occurring *P. vitticeps* that have much larger body mass and more sturdy bone structure than most inland dragons. These animals were imported to Germany in the 1980s, and the name German giant was applied. Since then, professional breeders have put great emphasis on carefully breeding and enhancing the size and strength of these massive dragons. To put a German giant dragon into perspective, large adult giants are up to 50 percent heavier than standard adult dragons, and while an adult female inland dragon may deposit up to 25 to 28 eggs in a clutch, a German giant female may lay as many as 65 eggs. That's one big bearded dragon!

All of the above-mentioned dragons are bred under various names by various breeders, and a seemingly endless variety of mixtures is currently appearing in the pet trade: Sandfire x

Example of a light orange dragon.

lemon-fire, gold x red, blood-red x lemon-fire, etc. The list of mixtures and combination dragons goes on and on, and with every passing year, some new variety hits the market and may be sold under any number of names. Just as soon as the hobbyist can wrap her or his head around all the available varieties, something new will appear online and in the herp trade shows.

As you might expect, any of these selectively bred dragons is going to cost considerably more than their standard counterparts, depending on how rare and sought-after the new type of dragon is. For matters of expense, I recommend that all beginning hobbyists try their hand at a normal color phase dragon at first, before moving on to one of these enhanced varieties. If you discover that bearded dragon keeping just isn't your bag, there's no sense in having to give away or try to sell a very expensive dragon (which may take a very long time to sell) when you can easily give away a normal specimen and not lose too much money.

Chapter 8

The Lawson's Dragon

I personally favor the Lawson's dragon (*P. henrylawsoni*) as the best pet dragon among the beardie clan. This smaller cousin to the inland bearded dragon is attractive, manageable, and highly prolific in captivity. Able to thrive in smaller quarters and in communal terraria, these dragons can make an excellent choice for the beardie hobbyist who doesn't have enough room to accommodate the larger inland bearded dragon. While an entire book could be dedicated to the wonderful lizards, I'll spend the next few pages describing them and their needs in captivity as best I can.

Lawson's dragon is a much more terrestrial species than the more common bearded dragon.

The Name Game

Formally described by Wells and Wellington in 1985, the first of these dragons was collected 100 miles west of Richmond, Queensland in January of 1978. When initially imported into private collections in the United States, this unusual dragon was known far and wide under the moniker of Rankin's dragon, after the Latin nomenclature, P. *rankini*. This nomenclature would change back and forth over the next decade and a half, until the name P. *henrylawsoni* was finally agreed upon. The name was given in honor of the Australian poet and turn-of-the-century philosopher, Henry Lawson (1867-1922). Lawson's dragons are also sometimes encountered for sale under the erroneous name P. *brevis*. Some common names used for this dragon include Down's bearded dragon, the black-soil bearded dragon, the black-plains bearded dragon, the dwarf bearded dragon (not to be confused with P. *minor*), and Rankin's dragon.

Natural History

Found throughout central and western Queensland, the Lawson's dragon has a much smaller natural range than does its inland cousin, and its habits of movement are much different. While the inland dragon is semi- to strongly arboreal (perching on fence posts and in low branches, for example), the Lawson's dragon is much more terrestrial, favoring rocky outcroppings and open, sunny flatlands to any variety of perch or arboreal retreats. There are other behavioral differences. P. *henrylawsoni* shows greater tenacity at defending that territory; the males tend toward quicker and more violent displays of aggression when an interloper enters their domain.

The Lawson's Dragon favors dry, rocky scrublands and arid, open flats of rocky mounds and few trees or shrubs. Cool, dark crevasses and stony hideaways are the Lawson's dragon's preferred retreats, and it will not hesitate to bury itself in loose sand or rocky soil when a predator draws near. Insects of all types are on the Lawson's dragon's menu, as are fruiting shrubs and flowering plants. Small reptiles will also find themselves at the mercy of an adult dragon's jaws. Predators of Lawson's dragons include a wide range of snake species, as well as monitor lizards and large birds.

Description

The first noticeable difference between the Lawson's dragon and the inland bearded dragon is the Lawson's diminutive size. With a maximum snout-to-vent length of just under 5 inches (12.7 cm), an adult Lawson's dragon grows to roughly half the size of an adult inland beardie; a Lawson's dragon reaches only 10 to 12 inches (25.4 to 30.5 cm) in total length, while the inland dragon may grow to a whopping 22 inches (55.9 cm) long. Not only is the Lawson's dragon shorter than the inland dragon, but in girth and weight, it is also proportionately smaller.

Life Span

One of the only drawbacks to keeping the Lawson's dragon is their life span. Not as long-lived as their inland dragon cousins, these lizards may only live for six to eight years in captivity. That's roughly 25 percent less time than an inland bearded dragon. If you heavily breed your female Lawson's dragon, you can expect her life span to be cut short by at least one to two years, as the rigorous stressors of breeding can take a serious toll on the female dragon.

Even the beards of the Lawson's dragon are proportionally smaller and only just noticeable. When angered and cornered, a wild Lawson's dragon will puff out its cute, little beard, hold its mouth agape, and hiss at its attacker, just like all dragons will. Adult size is largely the same between individuals of both sexes, the male Lawson's dragon typically growing to be only ever so slightly longer than his female counterpart.

Perhaps the most charming difference between this miniaturized dragon and its larger kindred is its stunning pattern. Sporting a base coloration of coppery brown to burnished tan, this dragon's back is barred in light tan or sandy colored dumbbell shapes, which straddle the midline of the back and project outward down the animal's flanks. Upon reaching the tail, these dumbbell shapes become simple bands that extend almost all the way around the tail. The belly is pale cream to sandy colored. The head of the Lawson's dragon is more vibrantly patterned than that of P. vitticeps, as well, with bars and flecks of light tan splashed across the coppery head. Unfortunately, these vivid colors fade as the dragon matures, and at full adulthood, a great many Lawson's dragons sort of "go gray," or fade into a much more uniform tan coloration, which is still quietly attractive, though it does lack the former glory of the dragon's youth.

Purchasing a Lawson's Dragon

When it comes to acquiring a Lawson's dragon, all the rules of health, coloration, alertness, etc. that applied to the inland dragon still apply, and there are some additional things to consider. Australia has banned the exportation of virtually all of its native species, so it's fair to say that no "new" Lawson's dragons are entering the herp hobby. By "new," I mean that only those offspring sired by existing captive bloodlines will be offered for sale on the open market. This means three things. One, that a Lawson's dragon will command a higher price than a standard bearded dragon. Two, that as time passes, the numbers of Lawson's dragons offered for sale will likely diminish as bloodlines taper off (the ill effects of inbreeding will accumulate). Three, that unscrupulous breeders and herp merchants have and will continue to offer hybridized dragons (inland crossed with Lawson's) for sale under the pretense that the animals are pure-blooded Lawson's dragons.

If you are interested in purchasing a Lawson's dragon, you really have to do some research beforehand. Make sure that the dealer you are interested in purchasing from is honest and offers only the purest and most high quality Lawson's dragons. Does this merchant have records and data and a traceable bloodline for his or her Lawson's dragons? Think about this as a sort of beardie pedigree. If the dealer seems hesitant to give you the dragon's genetic history, it's likely that he or she doesn't know such history and may be dealing (either inadvertently or maliciously) in hybrid dragons. Often sold under the name "*P. vittikens*," which is a hybrid of the names of *P. vitticeps* and *P. rankini*, these fertile

The Many Names of Lawson's Dragon

The name for this species was in flux for many years, and some breeders and hobbyists still use the outdated names. If you see any of the following names, they almost certainly are referring to Lawson's dragon:

Pogona brevis

Pogona rankini

Black-plains dragon

Black-soil dragon

Down's dragon

Rankin's dragon

hybrids are prone to shorter life spans than the inland beardie or the Lawson's dragon. If you're going to pay a Lawson's dragon price, you deserve to get a true Lawson's dragon.

Second, you'll most likely have to place a preorder with a breeder at least a year in advance. Lawson's dragons always sell out quickly. Placing a preorder means that you'll put a deposit down on a dragon that has not yet hatched, essentially buying the rights to a baby dragon when it is ready. Though this may sound odd, bear in mind that a great many popular herp species are sold out well before the eggs even hatch.

Health Issues

Before purchasing a Lawson's dragon, you must consider what I will call here, the "poor constitution" of these lizards. While Lawson's dragons are much hardier than many pet lizards available these days, they do suffer from a variety of maladies that do not afflict the inland bearded dragons. As I previously mentioned, all legally sold Lawson's dragons are bred from a limited source of bloodlines, and, as the genes in these bloodlines become more and more exhausted, genetic defects are becoming more and more commonplace. Inflammation of the liver and lysis of the cells of the liver have recently been noted in a few specimens since the mid 1990s. While very little is known about this bizarre and fatal disease, it is known to be far more prevalent in captive populations of Lawson's dragon than in wild populations.

Lawson's dragons also seem much more prone to contracting and retaining internal parasite loads, such as coccidian parasites, nematodes, and

Some breeders have crossed bearded dragons with Lawson's dragons. The resulting offspring are often called "vittikins."

others. Suffering under these parasites for longer periods of time and taking longer to be cured by appropriate medications, these dragons need considerably more veterinary attention when they take ill. Symptoms of internal parasite loads are as described for the inland bearded dragon, and include protracted weight loss, listlessness, loss of appetite, runny stool, constipation, vomiting and chronic regurgitation, and jerky movements of the limbs. If you suspect your Lawson's dragon is suffering from an internal parasite load, take it to the vet immediately.

Of course, parasite loads do not simply materialize out of thin air. They may come from other herps kept in the same room, fixtures or décor taken from one terrarium and placed into the dragon's enclosure, or feeding your dragon a diet of small reptiles. Anoles and house geckos, which can make excellent sources of protein in the inland bearded dragon diet, are frequently carriers of small parasite loads. While a healthy inland dragon may not contract these loads, Lawson's dragons are far more susceptible to infection. Reptilian prey items, therefore, should not be offered to Lawson's dragons.

Care

Keeping the Lawson's dragon in captivity is considerably different than keeping the inland bearded dragon. For starters, Lawson's dragons, owing to their demure stature, may be housed in smaller enclosures. For example, an adult inland dragon should be housed in nothing smaller than a 125-gallon tank (473 l), while an adult Lawson's dragon may thrive with an equal degree of freedom to roam about in a 70-gallon (265 l) tank. Juveniles and hatchlings may be housed in a 10-gallon-sized (37.9 l) terrarium for the first six months of life. After this time, they should be upgraded to at least a 20-gallon "long" (75.7 l) terrarium—preferably larger.

The Lawson's dragon is considerably more terrestrial than its inland cousin and requires a greater floor space-to-height ratio in its captive environment. Outfit the terrarium with plenty of hide boxes, low perches, and rocks. It has been my experience, and the experience of many other keepers, that Lawson's dragons absolutely love to bask atop, crawl over, and perch upon rounded-topped stones. Large stones, however, can be heavy (possibly breaking the base glass of the terrarium), so acrylic or polymer stones may have to be substituted for the real thing. Garden shops and hardware stores sell decorative terra cotta or polymer stones which, though they are intended for yard decoration, make excellent basking spots and climbs in the Lawson's dragon terrarium.

Sand is the best substrate for Lawson's dragons.

Humidity

Lawson's dragons also prefer lower levels of relative humidity than inland bearded dragons. While an inland dragon can tolerate humidity in the 50 percent range, I recommend nothing over 40 percent for a Lawson's dragon. For this reason, specialized equipment, such as a dehumidifier, may be necessary, depending on the climate of your locale. Exhaust fans affixed to the lid of the terrarium are also useful in keeping air circulation high, while minimizing humidity buildup inside the terrarium. As you might expect, water dishes must also be kept very small in the Lawson's dragon terrarium, as large dishes of water will create excess humidity as the water evaporates.

Heating and Lighting

Lawson's dragons also have more intense heating and lighting requirements than do their inland cousins. Hailing from the north-central region of Australia, Lawson's dragons enjoy at least an hour more daylight every day than do some populations of inland dragons. As a result, these lizards require a longer period of UV exposure than do the inland dragons. At least five to six hours of unfiltered, real sunlight is preferable for the long-term health and longevity of these lizards, though such an extended period of sunlight is often impractical, as few hobbyists have the leisure to walk their pet dragon in the park for six hours out of each day. Make sure to offer at least 12 to 15 hours of UVA and UVB lighting each day.

Heating, as you might expect, must also be heightened for these lizards: maintain daily ambient temperatures of 85° to 95°F (29.4° to 35°C) , with basking spots that reach 100° to 104°F (37.8° to 40°C). Nightly dips in temperature should not be excessive; air temperatures of 75° to 78°F (23.9° to 25.6°C) are best, though a warmer spot must be maintained either by way of an undertank heating pad or a small ceramic heat emitter.

Fractious Dragons

Perhaps the most notable of captive-care differences between Lawson's and inland bearded dragons come in the form of behavioral variations. While male inland bearded dragons will head-bob, arm-wave, and engage in semi-aggressive behaviors prior to actually fighting another male, the same cannot be said for the Lawson's dragon. These slight reptiles make up in ferocity for what they lack in size. Rival males rarely hesitate to engage in outright combat. For this reason, males should never be housed together; if males are housed together—even in very large enclosures—violence between cagemates is virtually guaranteed. Males also tend to display much more aggression toward females during copulation as well, biting the female's neck and dragging her about the terrarium violently. Great care must be taken when breeding Lawson's dragons.

Substrate

The matter of substrates is a simple one in the Lawson's dragon terrarium: use only sand. While the inland bearded dragons may be housed on bark chips, shredded coconut husks, sand, or any other dry substrate, the Lawson's dragon is considerably more demanding. Very fine-grained non-silica sand is acceptable, though most experts agree that calcium carbonate sands, such as those manufactured specifically for the pet trade, are best for housing Lawson's dragons. As is true of the inland dragon, this layer of substrate should be deep enough to accommodate the dragon's burrowing behaviors. A depth of at least 3 to 4 inches (7.6 to 10.2 cm) of sand is plenty.

Hide Box

When it comes to hide boxes, the Lawson's dragon also seems to have different preferences than the inland variety. Virtually any style or type of hide is sufficient for the inland bearded dragon, just as long as it provides shelter and darkness. Lawson's dragons, however, seem to prefer tight-fitting hides that touch their bodies on all sides. I've seen Lawson's dragons refuse the same, spacious hides that inland dragons wouldn't hesitate to utilize. This curious need for tight-fitting enclosures can most likely be explained by the lizards' primary defense mechanism. In the wild, Lawson's dragons seldom venture far from a rocky crag or stony overhang, for when a predator draws near, these lizards will scuttle into the nearest narrow crevasse, puff up their bodies, and wedge themselves firmly between the two stones. The predator is left frustrated and hungry for a lizard that it cannot remove from the rocks. In order to feel adequately secure in the home terrarium, these lizards need at last one or two tight crags in which they could wedge themselves should danger draw near. Obviously, there is no threat of predators in captivity, but you can't explain that to the Lawson's dragon.

Despite these lizards' propensity for tight-fitting hides, I still provide my animals with multiple hides of various sizes. Clay pot halves and artificial logs will suffice, while cinder block halves make the best hides, for by suspending a heating lamp above the cinder block, the hide can double as a basking site. Make sure, however, to provide a sufficient hide that is well away from any source of heat so that your lizard may thermoregulate as it needs to.

Diet

The diet of the Lawson's dragon is similar to that of the inland bearded dragon. As adults, they will take less vegetation than a beardie.

Breeding

There is good news about breeding Lawson's dragons and there is bad news. The good news is that the pre-breeding conditioning methods and practices for the Lawson's dragon are identical to those described for the inland bearded dragon. The bad news is that the breeding habits of the Lawson's dragon are considerably different than those of the inland dragon, and special considerations must be taken to ensure that the breeding of your Lawson's dragon doesn't end in premature tragedy.

The proverbial "rabbits" of the beardie family, Lawson's dragons are one of the most prolific lizards on the planet, breeding virtually night and day during the mating season. So intense is this mating fervor, in fact, that a male, if given the opportunity, will quite literally mate the female to death; his constant biting, dragging her about, and rough copulation will take a very high toll on the female. If you wish to breed Lawson's dragons, you must either remove the female from the male's enclosure within a few days after mating behaviors are observed, or you must establish a harem of females for your male. By housing your male in a large enclosure with five or more females, you will ensure that each female will get a resting period between sessions of copulation. This harem setup will also ensure that the male's mating fever is more evenly distributed among the females, and that no single female is worn to a frazzle. Remember to provide ample space for each dragon and multiple basking sites, hiding areas, and feeding stations.

Think Carefully

The captive breeding of the Lawson's dragon is not something that the casual hobbyist should engage in or take lightly. These animals cannot be imported from Australia, so all that exist in the pet trade are the offspring of a few captive bloodlines. By muddying or tainting those gene pools with hybridized or interbred specimens, the hobbyist may inadvertently contribute to the demise of these wonderful lizards in the pet trade. Help protect the current bloodlines of Lawson's dragons by engaging only in responsible, well-thought-out captive breeding projects.

A careful eye and quick wits are also required on the part of the keeper during the mating period, as even one mating can result in a torn and ragged female dragon. For this reason, it is best to keep a sharp eye on your male at all times and to keep plenty of hides available so that the females may find safe retreat from the passions of their overzealous tankmate. If one of your females does get injured, remove her from the breeding colony and tend her wounds appropriately.

A modified version of the harem setup is to establish a number of female dragons in separate enclosures, and simply move the male from one enclosure to the next on a rotating schedule. Many hobbyists have met with great success and minimal injuries by transferring the male from one terrarium to the next every 24 hours. This gives the male plenty of time to "take care of business," while not subjecting the female to prolonged attacks and periods of rough copulation.

Further proof of the overwhelming fecundity of the Lawson's dragon is seen in both the number of eggs deposited in each clutch and the number of clutches that a mature female may deposit each mating season. Females three to four years old may deposit as many as 27 to 30 eggs in a clutch, and may clutch up to five or even six times in a season. That's 180 Lawson's dragon eggs from a single female in a single year!

Unfortunately, Lawson's dragon eggs have a surprisingly low hatch rate when compared to those of the inland bearded dragon. If, for example, 100 eggs were laid by a female Lawson's dragon in a season, no more than about 85 are likely to hatch. This low hatch rate is seldom the fault of the keeper, nor is it the result of an unacceptable incubator. It is just the nature of these dragons to deposit a high number of slugs, duds, and otherwise unhealthy eggs in each clutch. Proper pre-conditioning, diet, exercise, and calcium/mineral supplementation can help to keep the number of these duds down to a minimum, but the hobbyist must be ever vigilant to keep a keen eye on the incubating eggs and remove any infertile or dead eggs as soon as they are apparent.

Once the eggs are deposited and all the slugs rooted out, the incubation period may last anywhere from 65 to 90 days, depending on the temperature at which you incubate the eggs: 82° to 86°F (27.8° to 30°C) is an acceptable range, with a constant 84°F (28.9°C) being ideal. Maintain a relative humidity of 75 to 85 percent inside the incubator.

Raising the Hatchlings

Once the eggs hatch, another, somewhat more gruesome difference between the Lawson's dragon and the inland dragon will become apparent. While hatchling inland bearded dragons can be housed communally for several weeks or even several months after hatching, Lawson's dragons *absolutely cannot be housed together after hatching*. Infamous among hobbyists for their cannibalistic nature, baby Lawson's dragons are born with a big appetite and an instinct to eat their own brothers and sisters! Even in as short a time as 48 to 72 hours after emerging from their eggs, the baby Lawson's dragons will begin attacking and eating one another. Nipped toes, bitten-off tails, and even full-body consumption will take place, for once a baby is bleeding and injured, the rest of the ghoulish brood will close in for the kill. While these cannibalistic fatalities are not common, they are known to occur.

This cannibalistic drive will remain until the young Lawson's dragon is at least four to six months old. After they have matured to this point, the young no longer see one another as a food source. The best way to avoid your dragons eating and being eaten by one another is to house them in separate enclosures from the moment they hatch.

Neonates are 1.5 to 2 inches (3.8 to 5.1 cm) long at hatching, and, if fed properly, will grow rapidly (even moreso than an inland dragon) until they reach sexual maturity at the age of 10 to 11 months. As is true of the inland bearded dragon, female Lawson's dragons are better off not breeding in their first year of life. By waiting until the female is in her second year of life before you breed her, you help ensure her continued health, and you reduce the potential for slug eggs to be deposited in each clutch.

All things considered, a Lawson's dragon can make an excellent pet. Though they are a little more difficult to care for, and their breeding habits are somewhat different, these lizards are still a great choice for the more advanced hobbyists among us. With a little time, care, and understanding, the Lawson's dragon can make just as satisfying and rewarding a captive as the inland bearded dragon.

CLUBS AND SOCIETIES

Amphibian, Reptile & Insect Association
Liz Price
23 Windmill Rd
Irthlingsborough
Wellingborough NN9 5RJ
England

American Society of Ichthyologists and Herpetologists
Maureen Donnelly, Secretary
Grice Marine Laboratory
Florida International University
Biological Sciences
11200 SW 8th St.
Miami, FL 33199
Telephone: (305) 348-1235
E-mail: asih@fiu.edu
www.asih.org

Society for the Study of Amphibians and Reptiles (SSAR)
Marion Preest, Secretary
The Claremont Colleges
925 N. Mills Ave.
Claremont, CA 91711
Telephone: (909) 607-8014
E-mail: mpreest@jsd.claremont.edu
www.ssarherps.org

VETERINARY RESOURCES

Association of Reptile and Amphibian Veterinarians (ARAV)
P.O. Box 605
Chester Heights, PA 19017
Phone: (610) 358-9530
Fax: (610) 892-4813
E-mail: ARAVETS@aol.com
www.arav.org

RESCUE AND ADOPTION SERVICES

ASPCA
424 East 92nd Street
New York, NY 10128-6801
Phone: (212) 876-7700
E-mail: information@aspca.org
www.aspca.org

Las Cruces Reptile Rescue
www.awesomereptiles.com/lcrr/rescueorgs.html

New England Amphibian and Reptile Rescue
www.nearr.com

Petfinder.com
www.petfinder.org

Reptile Rescue, Canada
http://www.reptilerescue.on.ca

RSPCA (UK)
Wilberforce Way
Southwater
Horsham, West Sussex RH13 9RS
Telephone: 0870 3335 999
www.rspca.org.uk

WEBSITES

BeardedDragon.com
www.beardeddragon.org

Beardie Resource Page
www.lizardheaven.com/resource.htm

Federation of British Herpetologists
www.F-B-H.co.uk

Herp Station
http://www.petstation.com/herps.html

Kingsnake.com
http://www.kingsnake.com/beardeddragons

Melissa Kaplan's Herp Care Collection
http://www.anapsid.org/

Reptile Forums
http://reptileforums.com/forums/

Reptile Rooms, The
http://www.reptilerooms.org

Tosney's Bearded Dragon Care
www.biology.lsa.umich.edu/research/labs/k
tosney/file/BDcare

MAGAZINES

Herp Digest
www.herpdigest.org

Reptiles
P.O. Box 6050
Mission Viejo, CA 92690
www.animalnetwork.com/reptiles

Reptilia
Salvador Mundi 2
Spain-08017 Barcelona
Subscripciones-subscriptions@reptilia.org

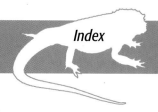

Index

Note: Boldface numbers indicate illustrations.

abscesses, 86
acrylic terrariums, 32
adoption of adult bearded dragon, 27
adult bearded dragon as pets, 26–27, **26**
adults, feeding of, 63–65
Agamidae family of lizards, 7
age and breeding, 95–96
aggressive behaviors, 53–55, 98, 120
albino bearded dragon, 110
amount to feed, 58
arm waving behavior, 14–15

banded bearded dragon. *See Pogona nullarbor*
bark as substrate, 38
beards, 14
behaviors, 14–16, 21–22
　aggressive, 53–55, 98, 120
　mating behaviors and, 98–100
　Pogona henrylawsoni and, 120
　territoriality and, 52, 53–55
billowing behavior, 17, **17**
bites from bearded dragon, 72
black-plains bearded dragon. *See Pogona henrylawsoni*
black-soil bearded dragon. *See Pogona henrylawsoni*
blood-red bearded dragon, 110
bone disease, 87–88
breeders of bearded dragon, 23–25
breeding, 93–111
　age for, 95–96
　aggressive behavior and, 98
　brumation and, 97–98
　gravidity and, 100–101

hatching of eggs following, 105–106
incubation of eggs and, 103–105
mating behaviors and, 98–100
nesting behaviors and, 100–103
Pogona henrylawsoni and, 121–123
pre-breeding conditioning for, 96–97
selective, and color varieties, 108–111
sexing of bearded dragon for, 94–95, **95**
slugs or unfertilized eggs from, 101
sperm retention and, 96
brumation, 97–98, **97**
burns, 78–79

cage liners, 37
calcium in diet, 59–60, 87–88
carpeting as substrate, 36
children and bearded dragon, 74–75
cleanliness and health, 87
coastal bearded dragon. *See Pogona barbata*
color varieties of bearded dragon, 108–111
conditioning for breeding, 96–97
crickets as prey items, 65–66
cryptosporidiosis, 82

digging a nest, **90**
Down's bearded dragon. *See Pogona henrylawsoni*
Drysdale River bearded dragon. *See Pogona microlepidota*
dwarf bearded dragon. *See Pogona henrylawsoni*
dwarf bearded dragon. *See Pogona minor*
dystocia, 88–90, 101

egg binding (dystocia), 88–90, 101

feeding, 57–67
　adults and, 63–65
　amount to feed in, 58
　gut-loading in, 59, 91
　hatchlings and, 61–63, 107–108
　illness/injury support and, 90–91
　insects to avoid in, 66
　juveniles and, 63
　natural diet and, 58
　obesity and, 89
　prey items in, 58, 65–66
　processed and canned foods in, 58
　record keeping in, **64**
　refusal to eat and, 67
　schedules for, 61–62
　spinach type plants in, 61
　vegetable matter in, 58
　vitamin toxicity and, 88
　vitamins and minerals in, 59–60, 87–88
　water and, 67
fences for outdoor enclosures, 51–52
furnishing your terrarium, 39–40

German giant bearded dragon, 110–111
glass terraria, 32
gold bearded dragon, 109, **109**
gravidity, 100–101
grooming your bearded dragon, 75
gut-loading, 59, 91

handling your bearded dragon, 20, 22, 69–73
　bites and, 72
　children and, 74–75
　do's and don'ts of, 70–72
　hatchlings and juveniles, 70

Photo Credits:

Marian Bacon: 1, 18, 30, 43, and front cover
J. Balzarini: 56, 74, 79, 83, 84
R. D. Bartlett: 10, 117
Adam Black (courtesy of The Gourmet Rodent): 22, 81, 97, 99, 105, 108, 111
Allen R.Both: 76, 119
I. Francais: 3, 16, 17, 20, 32, 34, 36, 40, 42, 45, 59, 61, 62, 65, 66, 70, 71, 72, 90, 92, 101, 102
P. Freed: 11, 55, 87
U. E. Friese: 28, 50, 53, 54
Erik Loza: 52,
G. and C. Merker: 6, 24, 37, 48, 107, 109, 112, 114
J. Merli: 14, 60
Gerald E. Moore: 68, 96
K. H. Switak: 7
Maleta M. Walls: 4, 15, 26, 38, 80, 86, 95, and back cover